*The Wealth and Income of the
People of the United States*

HISTORY OF AMERICAN ECONOMY

Editor-in-Chief: William N. Parker

YALE UNIVERSITY

The

Wealth and Income

of the

People of the United States

By Wilford Isbell King

With a New Introduction by
SOLOMON FABRICANT
PROFESSOR OF ECONOMICS
NEW YORK UNIVERSITY

Johnson Reprint Corporation

New York and London

1969

The edition reproduced here was originally
published in 1915.

Library of Congress Catalog Card Number: 69-20269

Printed in the U.S.A.

INTRODUCTION

With his book on the wealth and income of the United States, Willford King established himself among the pioneers in an area now busily cultivated by statisticians, economists, and historians. No scholar concerned after 1915 with the quantitative aspects of economic development in the United States could fail to start with the measurements King had made, if only to quarrel with the estimates before trying to adjust or replace them. The book is important in the history of American social science. 1991487

It is difficult for students of the present generation to appreciate the originality of King's book. Nowadays we are accustomed to having at our elbows the Bureau of the Census' *Historical Statistics of the United States* and its companion volume on *Long-Term Economic Growth,* both chock-full of information on income and wealth, and alongside them the annual *Statistical Abstract* to keep the series up-to-date. For information on other countries we need stretch a hand only a bit further to the latest United Nations *Yearbook of National Accounts.* Every year brings to our desks another volume of studies in the series published by the Conference on Research in Income and Wealth in the United States, or its sister conferences in other countries, or the International Association for Research in Income and Wealth; and the International Association now issues a quarterly *Review of Income and Wealth.* We no longer marvel at the array of income and wealth

data in Clark's *Conditions of Economic Progress,* and
take it for granted that the latest volume from the pen
of Kuznets, on *Modern Economic Growth: Rate, Struc-
ture and Spread,* will further widen our collection of
facts and deepen our understanding of them.

Nor is this all. In today's professional conferences and
journals are discussed not only the "plain and simple
facts" of the level, trend, and distribution of national
income and wealth. On the agenda are also input-output
matrices, flow-of-funds tables, and national balance
sheets, which trace more deeply interindustry and inter-
sector income and wealth relationships. The specialists
among us debate the problems of combining all these
measurements into an elaborate system of interlocking
national accounts, and of using the system to describe,
analyze, and control economic change. Only less com-
plicated are the "aggregate production functions," which
relate change in national income to change in wealth
and other variables, and on which econometricians pour
out papers. Even historians now try to read and use
these technical reports, for no one interested in the
process and sources of growth in national income can
afford to neglect any of the information that is being
amassed.

Yet only a few short decades ago, this body of information hardly existed. The "fancier" data are of
recent origin, of course. But even basic estimates of
income and wealth were few and far between, prior to

World War II. In the United States official estimates came in 1934, after the Senate had asked for a report on national income during the depths of the Great Depression. Only about seven other countries had official estimates of national income prior to World War II. In Britain, where national income concepts and measurement originated in the seventeenth-century work of Sir William Petty, no official or other regularly published estimates of national income were available until World War II was already under way. It took the needs of war-time planning, and the persuasiveness of Keynes, to make it possible for Stone and Meade to begin their work, although the depression and the publication of Keynes' *General Theory* in 1936 had already pushed national income into the mainstream of economics. It was the rise and spread of national economic planning after World War II that finally made the measurement of national income, and the other quantities to which King's book is devoted, a worldwide and continuous activity. The latest figures on national income are now front-page news, and we are beginning to expect even high school students to understand them.

The few estimates of income and wealth available before 1915 were all unofficial, and were usually for a single year only. They were prepared by different individuals on different occasions. They often differed in concept and method. The incomparabilities between the estimates of different years were usually serious, and determination of rates of growth difficult. In fact, not until King's book was published did any country possess a set of estimates covering a period as long as 1850–1910 and following reasonably consistent concepts and methodology. In Germany, for example, Karl Helfferich's estimates for 1896 to 1912, although published in 1913, related only to personal incomes, covered just Prussia, and fell far short of King's in accuracy and detail, as well as length of period covered. In Britain, no attempt at anything like a continuous historical series of estimates was made until those by Lord Stamp and A. L. Bowley, when King's book was already out.

King's book is remarkable also for the variety of approaches to national income measurement which he considered. His primary method involved determining the value added by production in each industry and combining these values to get a national total. But he also tried the finished-product approach, by summing up consumption estimates. The results obtained checked closely enough with the value-added approach to indicate "that a sufficient expenditure of effort might result in arriving at a close approximation to the money value of the goods used up in each year—a judgment borne out in the 1930's by the estimates made by Lough and Gainsbrugh, Warburton, and Kuznets. For 1910 King tried, in addition, the income-received approach, multiplying the estimated (or guessed) average family income in each class of the population by the number of families. In this case, too, the totals were not too distant from those obtained by the value-added approach, but he concentrated on the latter as conforming "far more closely to the limits of existing reliable data."

In the course of his discussion of methodology, King touched on questions that continue to trouble producers and users of national income statistics, and especially historians concerned with long-term changes. He referred to the value of housewives' services, which he felt should be included, but for which no statistics were available. He pointed to the bias caused by this and other omissions as production was transferred from home to factory. He mentioned the disappearance of the services of free goods, which also makes for an overstatement of economic growth. It is true, on the other hand, that King did not make any of the distinctions between national income at factor cost and net national product at market price, and between net and gross national product, which came into the literature a quarter-century later. Also, his terminology sounds "old-fashioned" to our ears, with "national dividend" standing for what is now called "national consumption," and "active capital" for today's "fixed business capital goods." Stranger is King's identification of his measurements by the years when the censuses were taken, rather than by the years covered by the censuses, which were largely the preceding calendar year. On the whole, however, King had a clear and rather modern view of what he was after when he measured income and wealth.

Another outstanding characteristic of King's book is

its comprehensiveness. He estimated not only the aggregates of national income and wealth but also their composition and distribution. And he assembled estimates of other quantities, such as productivity and wages, which he recognized to be important. In later years, these became the subjects of full-scale monographs by others.

It is not surprising, after a half-century, that these and the other estimates made by King have been very largely superseded by the results of later work. We now know that King overstated the long-term rate of growth of real national income; that real income per capita did not decline between 1860 and 1870, as his estimate suggested; that real wages in manufacturing rose, rather than leveled off, between 1890 and 1910, and that the wholesale price index which his limited resources forced him to use was a poor substitute for the deflaters he needed.[1] What is surprising is that not all of King's calculations are obsolete. His estimates still continue in use as building blocks in current estimates of the func-

[1] See Simon Kuznets, *Capital in the American Economy, Its Formation and Financing,* National Bureau of Economic Research, Studies in Capital Formation and Financing, No. 9, Princeton, Princeton Univ. Press, 1961; R. E. Gallman, "Gross National Product in the United States, 1834–1909," in Conference on Research in Income and Wealth, *Output, Employment, and Productivity in the United States After 1800,* Studies in Income and Wealth, Vol. 30, New York, National Bureau of Economic Research, 1966; and Albert Rees, *Real Wages in Manufacturing, 1890–1914,* National Bureau of Economic Research, general series No. 70, Princeton, Princeton Univ. Press, 1961.

tional distribution of income in the United States in 1910 and earlier years.[2]

Precisely because King's estimates are still in use, his book remains subject to criticism for failing to specify in detail the sources and methods he used in making his estimates. Comparing King's standards of documentation with those of today, critics complain that he did not follow closely what Goldsmith calls the "principle of reproducibility."

The charge is true, yet the criticism is not entirely warranted. It should be realized that King was severely limited in the assistance he had in his pioneering task and could not meet standards he himself would have liked to meet. As he states, a detailed description of sources and methods would have required several volumes, at a prohibitive cost. Also, King knew his figures were important and aimed his discussion at "every reader of good education." He preferred not to make his study intelligible only to "the technical student of statistics."

It is noteworthy, however, that King felt that even the general reader should be aware of the limitations of the estimates. He was therefore quite frank in stating that "the estimates have been made, in most instances,

[2] E. C. Budd, "Factor Shares, 1850–1910," in Conference on Research in Income and Wealth, *Trends in the American Economy in the Nineteenth Century,* Studies in Income and Wealth, Vol. 24, Princeton, Princeton Univ. Press, 1960.

from fragmentary material gathered by different persons at different times and for different purposes. . . ." and that "in some cases, details were filled in by the use of careful guesses based on general information only." "Whenever possible," he stressed, "the major conclusions have been verified by independent methods and from different sources of information." Because he claimed no absolute accuracy, he took care to specify a range of error, as in the first footnote to his summary Table XXI. And because he was uneasy about the apparent decline in real income per capita between 1860 and 1870, for example, he noted the possibility that the 1870 Census had been understated.

In a word, King knew that his estimates were approximate. He was aware that his documentation was scanty. He appreciated the need to improve both.

It might be added that rough as were King's estimates, and brief his notes, they would probably compare favorably in accuracy and documentation even with today's estimates in many countries of the world. It is certain, in any case, that King covered more ground, prepared and tested his results more carefully, and supported his estimates with more evidence than did his predecessors and most of his contemporaries. King stood at the divide, in 1915, between the "political arithmeticians" who raked figures together quickly to meet the needs of the moment, and the statisticians of the present age, who can demand and usually obtain the resources required for painstaking work.

King's standards are indicated not only by what he did and said in his book, but by his subsequent actions. When the National Bureau of Economic Research was organized in 1920, the first task on which it embarked was the preparation of estimates of national income in the United States for 1909–1919. King was invited to join the National Bureau's staff, and when he did, he shouldered a major part of the work. On its completion, he went on to advise in the National Bureau's study of the distribution of incomes by states, to assist the U. S. Bureau of the Census in planning its decennial report on national wealth in 1922, and to prepare for the National Bureau a thorough revision of its earlier income estimates back to 1909, and their extension through the 1920's. Later, when the National Industrial Conference Board began its series of studies of national income in the United States since 1799, King opened his work sheets to Martin, the investigator in charge, and gave him the benefit of his advice.

King expected his own estimates to be displaced by later estimates. I rather suspect that he was surprised to learn that any portion of his early estimates had survived long enough to be discussed in the 1957 joint sessions of the Economic History Association and the Conference on Research in Income and Wealth. But all of the work King published in 1915 survives in the sense that it paved the way for the later massive studies by the National Bureau of Economic Research, the Brookings Institution, the National Industrial Conference Board, and the Department of Commerce, and for the elaborate studies by individual scholars as well—from Douglas' on wages, to Gallman's on nineteenth-century national income.

In another respect, also, King's book marks a divide. Studenski pointed out in his history of national income estimates that "King concluded his estimate with a set of generalizations . . . derived more from his conservative philosophy than from the figures themselves. . . . King's was one of the last national income estimates in any country to combine the estimating task with economic politics." Many modern readers will not like King's "conservative philosophy." They will find curious, to put it mildly, his references to the "yellow peril" and the "white peril" in his comment on the effect of immigration on the wages of unskilled workers—though it is only fair to add that he may have been led to make a comment by his incorrect estimate of the trend of real wages during 1890–1910. And even today, when "population pressure" is becoming a respectable idea again, readers may raise their eyebrows at remarks—also applied to the problem of immigration, but in the United States of 1915—that "the law of diminishing returns is inexorable," and "inventions and discoveries may postpone but they cannot avert the day of reckoning."

But whatever our generation may feel about King's conservative views and his "economic politics," they were the views and the politics of a scholar "vitally interested in increasing man's share of the material things in life," as T. E. Murphy said in his biographical note in *The American Statistician* after King's death in 1962. "His goal was to improve the lot of mankind . . .; to benefit all of society and not any particular segment thereof." King's work on income and wealth, and his later work on hours and earnings, on the economic aspects of philanthropy, on savings, on index numbers, and on business fluctuations—all this scientific work was meant to serve his high purpose. King "may at times have been misunderstood," Murphy acknowledged, but "his unbending honesty of purpose was never challenged."

Solomon Fabricant

THE WEALTH AND INCOME

OF THE

PEOPLE OF THE UNITED STATES

THE WEALTH AND INCOME

OF THE

PEOPLE OF THE UNITED STATES

BY

WILLFORD ISBELL KING, Ph.D.

INSTRUCTOR IN STATISTICS IN THE UNIVERSITY OF WISCONSIN

NEW YORK

THE MACMILLAN COMPANY

LONDON: MACMILLAN & CO., Ltd.

1915

PREFACE

ABOUT a year and a half ago, the author had occasion to make a brief study of the national dividend in the United States; its size both absolutely and in comparison with the dividends of one or two European countries; and the possibilities of its increase. Professor Richard T. Ely listened to the reading of the paper and later saw fit to incorporate it as an appendix to his able work on *Property and Contract in their Relations to the Distribution of Wealth.* Professor Ely also suggested that the topic was one of sufficient importance to warrant its expansion into a small volume. The suggestion was accepted and, since that time, the original study has been thoroughly revised and decidedly extended. The author is indebted to Professor Ely for many helpful suggestions and criticisms, to Mr. Ray S. Trent, of the University of Wisconsin, for much assistance in collecting and compiling data, and to several students of statistics for preliminary work, necessary in clearing the way for some phases of the study. Mrs. Ray S. Trent, Mr. Robert C. Williamson, Mr. Reuben V. Gunn and Mr. Kenneth Duncan have given valuable assistance by reading and criticizing portions of the manuscript.

The reader of this book will do well to bear in mind that there are two broad varieties of concrete statistical studies: first, those depending on the correct counting of many individual items; second, those consisting of estimates based on counts made by others. This study is distinctly in the latter class. The estimates have been made, in most instances, from fragmentary material gathered by different persons at different times and for different purposes. In some cases, the original counts (principally by government officials) were doubtless faulty, but only when the errors were evident has the author attempted to go behind the returns and criticize the validity of government reports. Frequently, estimates have been made on the basis of assumptions that are possibly decidedly erroneous. In some cases, details were filled in by the use of careful guesses based on general information only.

The critics will immediately assert that such methods are useless and that the results are not worth the paper upon which they are printed. To this view the author takes exception. The primary value of statistics is usually due to relative rather than to absolute accuracy. It is believed that the figures cited are, in most instances, sufficiently accurate to justify fully the conclusions made concerning relative sizes, amounts, or changes. An effort has been made to state fairly the probabilities of error in each case and to convey in no instance any false impression of exactitude. The greatest possibilities of error are usually in the less important details and errors of this kind seldom can be great enough to vitiate seriously the totals arrived at. Whenever possible, the major conclusions have been verified by independent methods and from different sources of information. The closeness with which most of these independent estimates have checked has frequently been both surprising and gratifying.

The general sources of information and methods of procedure have usually been indicated either in the text or in a footnote. It has seemed unwise to attempt to trace in full all the methods used, for they have been so diverse and involved that their description in detail would require several volumes as large as this one. Neither has any attempt been made to give exact page references to all reports used. Figures have been taken from dozens or even hundreds of places in many of the sources cited, and to state the origin of each number would be to make the work so cumbersome as to discourage the average reader. This study is intended to give an impressionistic picture of the subject under consideration and to convey a correct idea as to the general supply and distribution of wealth and income. While no little effort has been expended in estimating and reëstimating, checking and rechecking with a view to

obtaining a degree of accuracy consistent with the
time and materials available and sufficient for the
purposes involved, in most parts of the book, there
has been no attempt made to render the details exact
or to enter into minutiae.   The author has sought to
make his ideas clear to every reader of good education
rather than to present a study intelligible only to the
technical student of statistics.   It seems quite certain
that it is absolutely impossible from the sources at
hand to construct a technically accurate statistical
answer to the questions about wealth and income
concerning which the thinking public wish information.   Numerous monographs and great bulky volumes of figures have been skilfully prepared which
admirably cover various phases of the question.
The author knows of no serious attempt, since that
made by Dr. C. B. Spahr some two decades ago, to
coördinate these studies into a connected whole.
Separately, they are of practically no value to the
ordinary citizen.   Yet these careful studies made
by the government or by independent workers at
great expense and effort contain hidden away therein
many broad truths which should be brought before
the public.   A knowledge of some of these facts is
necessary to enable one to determine the course of
political action which will best favor the advancement
of the nation.

The purpose of this book is to present some of these

important facts in a clear, comprehensible form. Its existence is justified exactly in the measure that this purpose has been attained.

WILLFORD I. KING.

THE UNIVERSITY OF WISCONSIN,
   April 17, 1915.

CONTENTS

CHAPTER I

LIST OF TABLES

1*

LIST OF DIAGRAMS

CHAPTER I

INTRODUCTION

I⊤ is a self-evident fact that the inventions and discoveries of the last two generations have revolutionized the productive forces of the American nation. In less than a century, the growth of population has changed a region consisting largely of a sparsely settled wilderness into a vast industrial empire. Our agriculture has made great advances, but the development of cities has been even more striking. All this has been so often told and retold that it has become the merest commonplace to every schoolboy. But when we come to a closer analysis of this tremendous advance, we find that even the principal features of the picture are far from clear. Everyone is aware that wealth has increased; most people feel sure that the average American of to-day is richer than the average American of fifty years ago; further than this, few can go with any degree of certainty.

But, in the present time of searching inquiry into the fundamentals of economics and politics, people wish to know more than this. They are not satisfied with the assurance that the accumulation of wealth within the nation is increasing. It is not enough to

2   1

know that the total income is greater than formerly. Nowadays, it is demanded that the economist bring forth a more complete picture of the change that has been going on. Many difficult questions are propounded. If wealth and income are increasing, is not population increasing faster? Is not the increase of wealth recorded in the statistical reports of our government merely an illusion arising from fluctuations in the supply of the medium of exchange? If there has been an increase in the riches of the nation as a whole, has the increase been distributed to all classes of the population, or have the benefits been monopolized by a favored few? Are the landlords, the capitalists, the captains of industry, or the wage-earners receiving the principal share of the fruits of progress? Each of these questions has been the subject of excited controversy, but, in the majority of instances, neither party to the debate has been able to reinforce his opinions with any evidence worthy of consideration, and hence it has been impossible to reach an agreement. The economist, in studying these questions, has been hampered by lack of statistical information on the subject. With the exception of Charles B. Spahr's work, entitled *The Present Distribution of Wealth in the United States,* all studies in this line have been admittedly incomplete and fragmentary. The book mentioned was published more than twenty years ago, and, in the interim, statistical science has made so much progress and government reports have become so much more accurate and complete that it seems possible and desirable again to attempt a study which will elucidate some of the questions mentioned above. As statisticians are well aware, the incompleteness of the earlier census reports, the lack of uniformity of the different censuses, and the absence of information on the exact points needed to throw light on the topics under discussion render futile, in the great majority of cases, any attempt to set forth authoritative or exact statements. The best that can be hoped for is to arrive at estimates near enough to the truth and with a small enough degree of error to make it possible to draw a few broad but practically certain conclusions.

As we approach the present time, the statistics become more and more complete and accurate, and, when we arrive at the censuses of 1900 and 1910, we may accept the results with a very considerable degree of confidence. Not only the Census Bureau but many other governmental departments have, in the last score of years, greatly increased both the quantity and quality of their statistical data. A study is, therefore, now rendered possible which covers in a general way a period of sixty years beginning with 1850. For the first few decades, only the broad outlines are trustworthy, but, as the end of the nineteenth century approaches, the facts become clearer and clearer and, after the advent of the Twelfth Census, one can proceed to analyze the figures in very considerable detail with a comfortable feeling of assurance that the results are approximately correct.

CHAPTER II

WEALTH

BEFORE beginning any investigation, it is absolutely essential that the problem to be solved shall be stated in such a form as to be perfectly clear and definite. What are the facts about which we wish to secure information? Since a number of problems are to be considered in the following pages, each will be stated separately in its proper place. These problems will deal mainly with wealth and income. Just what is wealth? How does it differ from income? Different authorities define these terms in various ways. The exact definition is not so important as is the necessity of adopting some clear-cut description of each term and then consistently adhering throughout to this meaning. The ideas embodied in the definitions which follow are intended to be as nearly as possible in accord with the best usage of the leading present-day economists. Since these economists do not agree on any set form of stating their ideas, the wording is that of the present author.

It has proved impossible to give any definition of the term **wealth** which does not include two distinct and yet overlapping ideas. Individuals are said to be wealthy when they possess bonds, notes, mortgages,

5

or stock in corporations. These evidences of title are, however, no part of the riches of the nation. If every paper of the sort were destroyed, the country, as a whole, might be little, if any, poorer. Its factories, stores, residences, farms, and mines would still exist. One citizen would have gained at the expense of another, but the total wealth of society might be practically undiminished. On the other hand, when a building burns the individual may be recompensed by insurance, but the loss is simply paid for by the policy holders in the company. The loss to society as a whole is approximately as great as if there had been no insurance whatever. Certain individuals may profit enormously by the increase in land values due to the growth of a great city, but the masses of the people will probably be forced by this same growth to travel far to their work or to live in crowded quarters amid the smoke and dust of busy thorough-fares. In this case, the individual wealth of a small fraction of the population has greatly increased, the wealth of the remainder of the inhabitants may also have increased if measured in dollars and cents, but, evidently, their real welfare has been decidedly diminished. The average of social well-being has fallen off. Economists, therefore, have found it essential to distinguish between the ideas of **private wealth, public wealth,** and **social wealth.**

Private wealth consists of material goods, claims

to such goods or to services, or evidences of those claims possessed by an individual or group of individuals at a given time. Thus, a man may own a farm, a store with an established business and good will, stock in a corporation, and greenbacks in his cash drawer. All these articles are part of his **individual wealth**. The United States Steel Corporation possesses mines, railways, ships and factories, as well as stocks and bonds of other corporations, monopoly privileges, etc. All these constitute the **corporate wealth** of the organization. Both **individual** and **corporate** wealth are forms of **private** wealth. The United States Government possesses thousands of public buildings, the great canal at Panama, fleets of ships, and vast quantities of valuable minerals and growing timber. In addition, it may own stocks, bonds, mortgages, and securities and it always has quantities of money of various kinds. All these things constitute the **public wealth** of the United States Government. Similarly, states, counties, cities, and townships possess many valuable things all included in a list of their public wealth. Evidently, public wealth differs from private wealth only in the point of ownership. We may, therefore, define public wealth thus: **Public wealth consists of material goods, claims to such goods, or to services, or evidences of these claims possessed by some governmental body or organization.**

The concept of **social wealth** is easy to define, not hard to grasp, but decidedly difficult to subject to measurement. The idea is thus set forth: **Social wealth consists of the aggregate stock of material goods possessed at the given time by the given segment of society.** Social wealth therefore is measured in **utility** and not in **value.** The value of the total stock of a commodity often increases as the quantity grows less, but total utility is likely to be greatly increased by abundance. Value is merely an exchange-ratio between different utilities. Only indirectly can value be used as a measure of social wealth, yet statistical inquiries concerning wealth are always made in terms of value. This fact renders difficult any bona fide comparison between wealth at different times and places.

Besides, only **economic** goods have value, that is only those goods which are too scarce to satisfy all wants for them. At the present time, this is, doubtless, a very important part of all goods, but it does not constitute the whole of social wealth by any means. Social wealth includes not only houses and lands, mines and live stock, farms and factories, clothing and furniture, but also the great mass of useful things generally known as **free goods.** Under this heading, we place seas, rivers, harbors, forests, climate, and scenery. Many of the richest treasures of mankind are free goods; that is, they exist so abundantly that all can share therein. A large fraction of the commerce of the world is carried upon the high seas, but there is no toll for the use of the ocean pathway. How much would the Mississippi valley be worth if its climate were arid? Yet, there is no charge for the rainfall. There is no price set upon Colorado sunshine or ocean bathing, but both have been important factors in contributing to American well-being.

Many authors have included as part of the social wealth the great stock of accumulated knowledge handed down to us by our forefathers and the intricate industrial, commercial, and governmental organization of society at the present time. The importance of these things cannot be overestimated. Without them, we should be compelled again to toil up the long tiresome incline from barbarism to modern civilization; yet it seems best to classify these not as wealth but as conditions making the accumulation of wealth possible. A man may be learned in the extreme and live amongst books representing the wisdom of the ages; he may dwell in a great industrial nation with a thoroughly modern form of organization; but if he owns no property he would not ordinarily be considered wealthy. Wealth, whether of persons or of nations, refers rather to actual accumulations of tangible things than to the power of amassing such riches.

Social wealth is commonly divided into three great categories which may be designated:

1. Productive Natural Resources.
2. Capital.
3. Consumption Goods.

Productive Natural Resources are varied in nature and character. Under this head, may be placed land including not only area, but soil, fertility, location, climate, and topography. Likewise, forests, stores of mineral resources, water- and wind-power, rivers, seas and oceans are all free gifts of nature which aid man in producing further wealth.

Social Capital includes all those products of past industry used in the further production of social wealth. It differs from **productive natural resources** in that labor has been involved in its production. It is not a free gift of nature for man has been compelled to use his brain and hands in assisting nature in order to make modern civilization possible. Capital is an intermediate product in the process of obtaining goods to satisfy human wants. It varies in nature and complexity from the sharpened stick with which the Indian woman planted corn to the giant press that prints a modern newspaper. As John Stuart Mill pointed out, all capital is the result of saving and in turn all capital is used up, but it is never used for the purpose of satisfying human wants directly. In so far as it does this, it loses its character as capital and becomes a **consumption good,** thus placing the article in the third category of social wealth.

Consumption Goods are those concrete goods at the service of the final consumer and intended for use in the satisfaction of human wants. Some consumption goods are free gifts of nature as the wild flowers on the hillside, the song-birds in the tree tops, the lakes, the mountains, and the waterfalls which make the landscape beautiful. Other consumption goods are the products of human toil coöperating with the forces of nature. Our houses and clothing, books and furniture, carriages and automobiles, food and fuel, all are the result of man's efforts and all yield directly an income of gratifications.

It is infinitely easier to classify wealth into logical categories than it is to measure the amount of wealth falling into each class. Wealth is a quantity of utility —of power to satisfy human wants. There exists, however, no standard unit of utility which may be statistically recorded by government officials, hence, we must adopt an indirect route and estimate wealth in terms of money value. This, unfortunately, rules out the consideration of free goods. No one can calculate the relative utility to the people of a nation of free as compared to economic goods. It is said that the food supply of some of the African tribes consists almost entirely of wild fruits growing in the forest. To them, free goods are doubtless more essential than economic goods. Free goods played an important rôle in the life of the American frontiersman. Wild game and fruit furnished much of his sustenance. He paddled his canoe along untrammelled streams, hunted in the primeval unowned forest, and cooked his food over a fire of free wood. The city dweller to-day, on the contrary, pays for almost everything he enjoys, except the air which he breathes and he has to pay dearly enough to live in a district in which the air is fairly pure. It does not, therefore, necessarily follow that because the **economic goods** owned by the city dweller of to-day possess twice the utility of the **economic goods** owned by his grandfather, the frontiersman, he possesses twice the wealth of his grandsire. The reverse may be true. This fact must be kept in mind when studying comparisons of the wealth of peoples widely separated in time or environment. Since no statistical measures of free goods are available, comparisons can be made only between **values** of **economic goods.** In recent times, when a larger and larger percentage of social wealth is becoming economic or scarce, measures of economic wealth become better and better criteria of the actual social wealth of a community or nation.

CHAPTER III

CHANGES IN THE SOCIAL WEALTH OF THE AMERICAN PEOPLE

SINCE we cannot measure the absolute utility of the wealth possessed at different dates by the people of the United States, we must seek for the best available criteria which may be used as approximate yardsticks or standards of measurement. The latest official figures available give the following estimates of the money value of the economic wealth of the American people.

TABLE I

THE MONEY VALUE OF THE ECONOMIC GOODS POSSESSED BY THE PEOPLE OF THE CONTINENTAL UNITED STATES.[1]		
Year.	Total Amount.	Amount per Capita.
1850	$ 7,135,780,000	$ 307.69
1860	16,159,616,000	513.93
1870	30,068,518,000	779.83
1880	43,642,000,000	870.20
1890	65,037,091,000	1,035.57
1900	88,517,307,000	1,164.79
1904	107,104,212,000	1,318.11

These figures indicate a tremendous growth in the possessions of the people, even when considered from the per capita standpoint. Before we can arrive,

[1] *Statistical Abstract of the United States for 1913,* p. 628; excludes Alaska and the island possessions.

however, at any definite conclusion we must consider the estimates critically. It is, of course, understood that the figures are more or less inaccurate, but any probable percentage of error is almost sure to be negligible in so far as accounting for the tremendous and steady increase appearing in the recorded amounts. Since, however, wealth is measured in utility and these figures are given in terms of value, we must, to the best of our ability, eliminate changes due to fluctuations in the purchasing power of the medium of exchange. We may, perhaps, be safe in assuming that the utility of a bushel of wheat or a yard of sheeting is approximately the same to-day as it was fifty years ago. By following the same line of reasoning, if we were to divide the wealth at a given date by an index[1] of the general level of prices, we should obtain a rough composite measure, in terms of weight or bulk or area, of the economic goods in existence at each date. This might, on the whole, answer fairly well as an indicator of the economic wealth at the different census years. One difficulty, however, immediately confronts us. A large part of

[1] For the information of those not versed in statistical science, it may be said that index numbers are used to compare numerical amounts as to their *relative* size. The basic quantity, to which all other quantities are compared, is, ordinarily, represented by 100. Thus, if the price of wheat in 1890 were 80 cents and if this price were taken as a base, or 100, then, in 1896, when the price of wheat fell to 60 cents, the index number would be 75. If, in 1910, the price rose to $1.20, the index number would be 150.

this increase in wealth is represented by rising land values and we have no index of prices including land in the list of commodities used in computing the index. We must, therefore, study the land supply separately.

THE LAND SUPPLY

The land supply may be considered either from the narrow point of view of the owner of the land or from the broader point of view of the people of the nation as a whole. It is from the productive resources given us by nature that we must all derive our sustenance—it is on the land that we must all find homes. In this study, therefore, we shall take the broader or social standpoint.

The land of the rural regions furnishes us with foodstuffs and raw materials. In the cities, land is principally valuable because of mere area—its power of supplying space for playgrounds, streets, homes, factories, stores, and office buildings. In the first instance, the quality of the land is of prime importance. In the second case, quantity and location are the principal requisites. We shall first discuss the changes in the supply of the latter variety—the urban land of the United States.

URBAN LAND

Agricultural land is doubtless one of the most essential of all the gifts which nature has bestowed upon the American people, but, while we must all eat, and, in order to eat, must depend on the products of farm land in the United States or elsewhere, we must also all have a place of abode. Most of us

TABLE II

CENSUS YEAR.	NUMBER OF FARMS IN THOUSANDS.[1]	POPULATION IN THOUSANDS.					PERCENTAGE OF POPULATION.			
		Total.[2]	Agricultural.[3]	Cities and Villages.			Agricultural.	Cities and Villages.		
				Under 8,000.[3]	8,000 to 100,000.[7]	Over 100,000.		Under 8,000.	8,000 to 100,000.	Over 100,000.
1850	1,449	23,192	9,418	10,877	1,504	1,393[5]	40.6	46.9	6.5	6.0
1860	2,044	31,443	12,674	13,697	2,447	2,625[5]	40.3	43.6	7.8	8.3
1870	2,660	38,558	15,430	15,056	4,126	3,946[6]	40.0	39.1	10.7	10.2
1880	4,009	50,156	22,049	16,789	4,927	6,391[6]	44.0	33.5	9.8	12.7
1890	4,565	62,948	24,652	20,023	8,575	9,698[4]	39.2	31.8	13.6	15.4
1900	5,737	75,995	29,834	21,169	10,784	14,208[4]	39.3	27.8	14.2	18.7
1910	6,362	91,972	31,810	24,409	15,451	20,302[4]	34.6	26.5	16.8	22.1

Table title: THE ESTIMATED RURAL AND URBAN POPULATION OF THE UNITED STATES (Exclusive of Outlying Possessions[8]).

[1] *Statistical Abstract of the United States for 1912*, p. 770.

[2] *Ibid.*, p. 41.

[3] Estimated by assuming that the average farm family has gradually decreased in number of persons from 6.5 in 1850 to 5.0 in 1910.

[4] *Abstract of the Thirteenth Census of the United States*, p. 59.

[5] *Eighth Census of United States*, pp. 242–244.

[6] *Tenth Census of the United States, Population*, pp. xxx–xxxi, 447–456.

[7] *Twelfth Census of the United States*, Vol. I, Pt. I, p. lxxxiii.

[8] Outlying possessions consist of Alaska, Hawaii, the Philippines, Porto Rico, the Canal Zone, etc.

to-day live in cities or towns or villages and we are just as much interested in the land we live upon as in the land which furnishes us with food. Let us, then, first consider the supply of residential land.

The farmer, in most cases, has as much residential land as he desires. His circumstances, in this respect, have probably not changed materially since 1850. The same cannot be said of the urban dwellers.

It is the practically universal belief that the last sixty years has witnessed a wholesale cityward migration of the farmers of the United States. We have been told over and over again that "the high cost of living" is due to the fact that the American farmer's sons have been lured away by the attractions of the city, leaving the rural regions relatively depopulated. An examination of Table II, Column 8, however, shows that the Census figures tell a very different story. The chief objection to the rural depopulation theory appears to be that no such depopulation has occurred. While millions of the boys and girls from the farms have yielded to the attractions of city life, many more millions have remained to cultivate the soil. In addition, a constant stream of immigrants from northern and western Europe has peopled great sections of the farming districts of the Upper Mississippi valley and the Great Plains. In 1850, 40.6 per cent. of our people lived on the farms and, at the close of the century, 39.3 per cent. still remained

3

there. Only in the last decade has the percentage of our population engaged in farming shown a marked decline. Yet the fraction of the population living in cities has steadily and rapidly increased. What is the explanation?

FIGURE 1

A CLASSIFICATION OF THE POPULATION OF THE UNITED STATES ACCORDING TO URBAN OR RURAL RESIDENCE.[1] 1850–1910

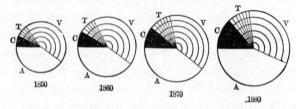

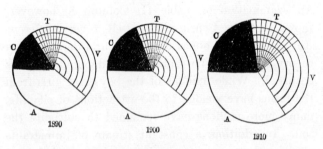

C   Cities over 100,000
T   Cities 8,000 to 100,000
V   Villages under 8,000
A   Agricultural Population

A glance at Fig. 1 and the ninth column of Table II answers the query. Our village population has been

[1] See Table II.

a relatively declining factor throughout the whole six decades. While the number of villagers has a little more than doubled, the city population has been multiplied by twelve. This does not necessarily mean that the villagers or their children have almost unanimously moved to the cities. Many have remained in their old homes and have watched the hamlet develop into a town and the town into a city and even the city into a metropolis. In addition, large numbers, probably, of the enterprising youths of the village have sought fortune or pleasure in the neighboring cities. But the greatest single source of city growth has been the deluge of foreigners who have gone to some American city directly from Europe and who have remained in the cities in such numbers that most of our great metropolitan centers now possess a majority of either the foreign born or their children.

It would require an exhaustive separate investigation to determine the exact causes of city growth and that is far outside the scope of this study. The fact that stands out clearly is that, while our farming population has almost kept pace with the general growth of the nation, the village growth has been relatively slow, and that every village loss in percentage of the total population of the country has been absorbed by the cities. As a result, each decade has seen a larger fraction of the American people living in a city environment. The large city has grown even faster than the small one. In 1850, only a paltry six per cent of our people dwelt in cities of over 100,000 inhabitants. To-day, such cities are the homes of nearly one-fourth of all our population. How has this change affected the supply of residential land per capita?

The villager is usually well supplied with land. His house is, ordinarily, surrounded by a lawn and has a garden at the rear. In the smaller cities also this is likely to be true, but, in the great metropolis, it is the rare exception. In general, therefore, the larger the city, the less of residential land is available for each family. It may, then, be safely said that the sixth part of our population, those who live in cities of from 8,000 to 100,000 inhabitants, are not quite as well supplied with land as under the village conditions of the past, while, for the nearly one-fourth of our people living in cities of over 100,000, the conditions are decidedly worse as regards available space for residence. The increasing crowding, which makes itself manifest by increasing rents and land values, has forced far too large a fraction of the inhabitants to dispense with every semblance of a grass plot or garden and to live in many-storied structures among the dust and smoke which so universally accompany the factory and business districts. Urban residence land-values have gone skyward, forcing the city dwellers into greater and greater congestion, in other words, into a more and more restricted use of land for the average person. The rise of the assessed value of land in a city is, then, far from being a mark of increased land supply— of better conditions of life for the average inhabitant. On the reverse, rising land values, in a city of over 50,000 people,[1] almost invariably signify a diminution of the benefits of land to the average citizen, and, since the urban dwellers now form such an important fraction of the entire population, a decrease in the average well-being of the American people in so far as the supply of residential land is concerned.

When it comes to land for business purposes, we find that the large cities have also a shortage in this line, especially in the retail and office districts. This is clearly evidenced by the great skyscrapers erected at a cost of so many millions in the down-town section of every large city. The disadvantages of land shortage, in this case, are largely offset by the advantage of getting related businesses close together and the resulting facilitation of large-scale industrial operations. The crowding of business into small areas may, therefore, be passed over as a form of land shortage which is slightly, if at all, detri-mental to the social welfare.

[1] As a village grows into a city, many improvements such as water-pipes, gas-mains, paving, etc., are incorporated into the land, thus giving added utility to offset the rising price.

Agricultural Land

In this connection, it must again be emphasized that we cannot measure land supply in terms of value. Rising prices of farm land only show that farm land is becoming more desirable as compared to money. But land is something which grows real material crops to satisfy our hunger. A bushel of wheat goes no further when it is worth a dollar than when it sells for fifty cents. In measuring the benefits of agricultural land we must, therefore, consider not its value but its area and fertility.

Table II showed us that, despite the general belief to the contrary, the fraction of our people engaged in farming has shown a remarkable constancy, only beginning to fall off materially during the decade 1900–1910. Since 1850, the number of farmers in the United States has more than trebled, but the area of the United States proper has remained almost unchanged. How has our growing farm population fared for land?

Table III brings out the fact that, as far as land acreage is concerned, the farmer is little worse off to-day than in 1850. The amount of land for each farm inhabitant has decreased only about one-ninth during this entire period. The great, fertile Mississippi Valley has been opened up and settled and, until recently, the Federal government gave farms for the asking to nearly everyone desiring land.

TABLE III

| | | ACREAGE OF FARM LAND PER PERSON. | |
CENSUS YEAR.	TOTAL ACREAGE IN FARMS.[1]	For Persons Living on Farms.	For All Persons in the United States.
	LAND IN FARMS IN THE UNITED STATES (outlying possessions excluded).[2]		
1850	293,560,614	31.17	12.66
1860	407,212,538	32.13	12.95
1870	407,735,041	26.43	10.58
1880	536,081,835	24.31	10.69
1890	623,218,619	25.28	9.90
1900	838,591,774	28.11	11.03
1910	878,798,325	27.63	9.55

But, in agriculture, acreage is not an accurate measure of land supply. During the period 1850 to 1885, the land brought into cultivation was, as a rule, of better quality than that hitherto farmed. The rich lands of Illinois and Iowa were equalled in fertility by no large area in the East. But, since 1885, there has been a marked change. The margin of cultivation, that borderland where it is just worth while to cultivate the soil, has come gradually to depend not upon railway facilities or distance from market but upon rainfall. Across the Great Plains, the farmer has pushed closer and closer to the base

[1] See the *Statistical Abstract of the United States for 1912*, p. 139, and *The Abstract of the Thirteenth Census of the United States*, p. 265. Land in farms includes pasture and woodland as well as cultivated fields.

[2] See Table II.

of the Rockies and, as he has done so, the difficulty of producing a bushel of corn or wheat has continually increased. He has resorted to irrigation and other devices unnecessary in the moist climate of the Valley and these all require greater effort in order to secure the same yield. But the precipitation, and hence the water supply, of the Western Highlands is scanty and, as a result, but a trivial fraction of the semi-arid plains can be irrigated. The great bulk of the farming must depend for moisture upon the rainfall directly provided by nature. This is, too often, light and irregular. Even with the most modern and approved methods of "dry farming", crop yields are apt to be small and crop failures or partial failures very frequent. We should naturally expect, therefore, to find the average quality of our farm land to-day to be poorer than the average quality of the farm land of a quarter century ago. This expectation is apparently fulfilled by an examination of the yields per acre of leading crops. Few will deny that, with the growth of scientific agriculture, with the multiplication of farm journals, agricultural schools, and experiment stations, our methods of farming have been improved. Plant breeding has given us more productive varieties of grains and vegetables and the farmer has been taught how to grow them. If, then, the average quality of farm land has not grown worse, a greatly increased yield per acre would be almost certain. Table IV shows us the actual condition of affairs for the last forty-seven years as reported by the United States Department of Agriculture.

TABLE IV

ACRE YIELDS OF LEADING CROPS IN THE UNITED STATES (outlying possessions excluded).[3]					
PERIOD.	AVERAGE CROP PER ACRE.[1]				
	Corn, Bushels.	Wheat, Bushels.	Oats, Bushels.	Barley, Bushels.	Cotton,[1,2] Bales.
1866–1875	26.1	11.9	28.1	22.9	—
1876–1885	25.5	12.3	27.6	22.4	.348
1886–1895	23.5	12.6	25.6	22.6	.383
1896–1905	25.2	13.5	29.6	25.1	.405
1906–1912	27.0	14.5	29.1	25.0	.394

From these figures, we see that, in every instance, these leading crops have shown an increased yield per acre. In the case of wheat and cotton, it is quite marked; in the case of corn, oats, and barley, it is very slight. On the whole, the increase appears to be less than we should have expected from the new methods of agriculture if applied to a constant quality of land. Apparently, therefore, the average farm land of to-day is not quite so fertile as the average farm land of a generation ago, but improved

[1] *Statistical Abstract of the United States for 1912*, pp. 143–145, 158, 772.

[2] *Statistical Abstract of the United States for 1899*, p. 372.

[3] See Table II.

methods of farming have led to an increased product per acre. In other words, the rich land reclaimed from swamps, cleared of stones and timber, or brought under irrigation has not been quite sufficient in quantity to offset the large tracts of semi-arid land recently added to our farm area. Since, to-day, the unoccupied or scantily settled portions of the United States lie mainly in the semi-arid West, we must anticipate in the future that the growth of population will cause the average quality of our agricultural lands steadily to grow poorer and poorer.

Up to the present time, however, the farmer cannot be said to have lost, materially, either in the area of land which he cultivates or in its quality. The benefits of land which have actually been lost to the farmer seem to consist principally of the services of the neighboring free land to which he formerly had unrestricted access though possessing no title thereto. The frontier farmer could hunt, fish, pasture his stock and cut timber on the unoccupied lands near his abode. These privileges cost him nothing. To-day such opportunities are becoming more and more rare. True, such privileges were always far from universal, but, in earlier times, they accrued to a much larger share of our rural population than is the case to-day. In this respect, then, the average farmer gets less of the advantages of land than formerly.

But, to consider farm land as it affects the farmer only, is a narrow and individualistic point of view. The agricultural lands of a nation are the heritage of the whole people. From these lands they must largely draw their supplies of food and clothing. The most pertinent query, therefore, is: "Has the supply of farm land increased as rapidly as the population of the United States as a whole?" We know that our population has grown tremendously while the geographical area of the continental United States has remained about constant, but much of the land was formerly unoccupied and yielded only a small product of game, timber, or pasture. Have we succeeded in carving out new farms at a rate to keep pace with our increasing numbers? A glance at the last column of Table III shows that, while we have failed in this respect, yet we are a surprisingly short distance behind in the race. Each inhabitant of the United States to-day has more than three-fourths as much farm land producing for him as had the inhabitant of 1850 and the loss since 1870 has been only about one acre per capita. There has, however, been a sharp decline since 1900 which apparently indicates that the difficulties of getting land suitable for farming are on the increase to such an extent as to portend a serious shortage for the future.

Grazing Lands

But farms and residence lots are not the only kinds of land. Not many years ago, ranches covered nearly half of the area of the United States. Throughout the West, great herds of cattle and sheep roamed over vast stretches of the public domain. To-day, the best of this territory has been occupied by farms and the ranchman has been driven back to the more barren sandhill or semi-desert regions. The growing cry for food has led the corn and wheat farmer to encroach upon the "cow-country"—to undertake a precarious fight against drought in the hope of wresting from unwilling nature a few more bushels of grain to satisfy the hunger of the oncoming millions. His invasion has proved a body blow to the cattle and sheep industry as is shown by Table IVA.

From 1880 to 1900, the number of cattle in the United States almost doubled, but, during the decade 1900 to 1910, the advent of the farmer in the range country and the higher prices for farm produce which led to the breaking up of pasture lands and the more extensive feeding of cut forage and grain caused a sharp decrease in the total number of cattle in the country. During the same period, population greatly increased so that the supply of cattle per capita diminished by one-fourth. Since the census year of 1910, the reports of the Agricultural Department indicate that the rate of diminution in the supply has greatly accelerated, and that in 1913 there were almost one-fifth less cattle in the United States than in 1910, the per capita decrease being more than that amount.* This fact has been abundantly evidenced by the rising prices of beef which threaten soon to eliminate steaks and roasts from the diet of the average American.

TABLE IVa

CENSUS YEAR.	CATTLE.		SHEEP.[4]	
	Total Number.	Number per Person.	Total Number.	Number per Person.
1880	39,675,533[1]	.791	42,000,000[1]	.84
1890	57,215,212[2]	.909	40,876,312[2]	.649
1900	67,719,410[3]	.891	61,503,713[3]	.809
1910	61,803,866[3]	.672	52,447,861[3]	.570
1913	50,572,000[5]	.521	47,193,000	.486

THE NUMBER OF CATTLE AND SHEEP ON FARMS AND RANGES IN THE UNITED STATES (outlying possessions excluded).

Sheep have shown a similar tendency with even more striking results. Despite the until recently continued presence of high protective duties on wool,

* *Statistical Abstract of the United States for 1913*, p. 770.

[1] *Tenth Census of the United States*, Vol. III, p. 141.

[2] *Eleventh Census of the United States, Statistics of Agriculture*, p. 29.

[3] *Abstract of the Thirteenth Census of the United States*, p. 311.

[4] Excludes most of spring lambs.

[5] Estimated from reports of United States Department of Agriculture.

FIGURE 2

NUMBER OF CATTLE AND SHEEP ON THE FARMS AND RANGES IN
THE UNITED STATES, PER INHABITANT[1]

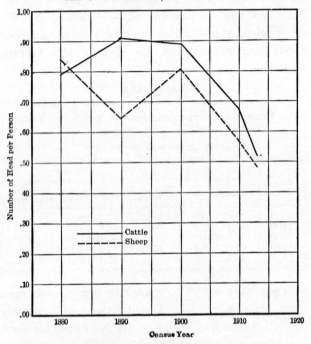

Note: Only years 1880, 1890, 1900, 1910, and 1913 significant—
straight lines between these points.

the sheep-grower has been unable, on the fertile
Eastern lands, to compete with the grain farmer and
the encroachment on his pasture land has gradually

[1] See Table IV.

forced him out of business. The decade 1900 to 1910 showed a falling off of over one-fourth in the per capita supply of sheep and the later figures of the Department of Agriculture show that in 1913 the movement was still going on at a similar rate.[1]

Thus, we perceive that the apparently satisfactory manner in which the area of our farm lands has kept pace with our population has not been quite so much a cause for self-congratulation as it at first appeared. Grain-farming has grown at the expense of grazing and the increase of our supply of agricultural land has been at the expense of our ranges. If events continue along the present trend, we seem destined to lose our proud boast that the American workingman has meat on his table three times a day. Despite our vaunted increase in wealth, one of the widely-accepted landmarks of prosperity will have disappeared.

FORESTS

Another important category of our natural resources consists of forests and the lands upon which they grow. When America was discovered, nearly one-half the area of the present United States was covered with fairly dense forests. At the present time, only about 300,000,000 acres of merchantable timber is left standing, one-third of this area belonging

[1] *Statistical Abstract of the United States for 1913*, p. 771.

to the National Government.[1]   The total forest area comprises less than one-sixth of the country as a whole.   Thus, nearly two-thirds of the original forests have been cleared off and it seems true, beyond question, that this includes decidedly the best two-thirds of the timber.   It is not, however, fair to assume that the timber removed represents a net loss in the natural resources of the country.   A large part of the cleared land is more valuable with the trees off than in its original state—that is, it is better suited to agriculture than to forestry.   We cannot have both on the same land and we have chosen the farm.   At the present time, however, the larger part of the land which is being cut over is not well adapted to agriculture.   When this is true, every acre denuded represents a net decrease in the wealth of the nation.   It is safe to say that, during the last score of years, the land cleared has had its utility diminished by the removal of the trees.   Hence, as regards timber, our national wealth, as represented by natural resources, is rapidly on the decline, so rapidly in fact that it is commonly asserted that ~~two~~-thirds of our best existing forests will have disappeared during the next two decades, those remaining being principally the wood lots of the farmers and the national forests protected by the United States

[1] Van Hise, Charles R., *Conservation of Natural Resources in the United States*, p. 210, and the Report of the Commissioner of Corporations on *The Lumber Industry, Part I, Standing Timber*.

Government. It is worth mentioning in this connection that certain railroad companies are now engaged in replanting large areas of cut-over lands in the hope of providing for a future supply of ties and stringers. This work, while as yet on a small scale, bids fair, in some slight degree, to offset the diminution in the social wealth of the nation due to forest removal.

MINERAL RESOURCES

It is a commonplace that the United States has been endowed with great mineral resources and that these gifts of nature have been rapidly "developed" or "exploited." Useful minerals are the product of long ages of geologic activity and, in the historical life of the nation, the amount of deposits formed has been negligible. When we rapidly "develop" our mines or oil wells, we are in the position of the spendthrift who inherits a fortune with the provision that it is to be paid to him in annual installments, but who, by some hook or crook, arranges to double the size of each installment. As a result, he lives, at present, in great affluence, but, when his estate is once squandered, he will be in poverty. Likewise, it is true of our mining operations that every ton of coal, every barrel of oil removed from the earth means an irremediable loss to our national estate. Each year, our social wealth, as represented by minerals, grows less and less and the

4

more flourishing the condition of our mining industry, the more rapid the disappearance of our mineral estate.

Coal is our most important mineral asset—the motive force of modern civilization. The amount in the ground in 1908 was estimated by the National Conservation Commission to be 3,135,708 million short tons.[1] The tremendous advance in exploitation during each decade is shown in Column 2 of Table V.

TABLE V

Year.	Coal in Millions of Long Tons.	Pig Iron in Thousands of Long Tons.	Copper in Thousands of Long Tons.	Phosphate Rock in Thousands of Long Tons.	Petroleum in Millions of Gallons.	Natural Gas in Millions of Dollars' Worth.
PRODUCTION OF IMPORTANT MINERALS IN THE CONTINENTAL UNITED STATES.[2]						
1850	6	564	0.7	—	—	—
1860	13	821	7	—	21	—
1870	29	1,665	13	—	221	—
1880	64	3,835	27	211	1,104	—
1890	141	9,203	116	510	1,925	19
1900	241	13,789	271	1,491	2,672	24
1910	448	27,304	482	2,655	8,801	71
1912	477	29,727	558	2,973	9,329	—

At the present **rate of increase** in mining, the stock of coal on hand would last only about a century and a half, but it is highly improbable that this present rate of increase will continue. At the present **rate of mining**, it would supply us for nearly seven thou-

[1] *Statistical Abstract of the United States for 1912*, p. 34.
[2] *Statistical Abstract of the United States for 1913*, pp. 773–775.

sand years. The actual time during which we can obtain coal, therefore, can only be guessed at, but it will probably be several centuries. The fact must not, however, be overlooked that we are now taking out the coal of first quality which is easy to reach. Much of the stock in the ground is of extremely poor grade or very difficult to mine. As a result, our social wealth in coal is diminishing much more rapidly than would be indicated by the actual number of tons mined as compared to the total supply. This same statement would apply with equal force to practically all of our other mineral resources.

The metals, unlike coal, do not entirely perish in the using but, to a large extent, are transformed from natural resources into capital goods, still being included as a part of our social wealth. Of course, large quantities are lost through oxidation and wear. In painting and gilding alone, huge amounts of lead and gold are placed in a form from which their re-collection as a mass of metal is impracticable. Nevertheless, the annual loss in our inventory of metallic ores is partially offset by an increase in the stock of refined metals on hand.

As estimated for the year 1912 by the National Conservation Commission, the total supply of iron ore of a quality profitable to mine was 4,784,930,000 long tons.[1] Of this, we are mining from forty to

[1] *Statistical Abstract of the United States for 1912*, p. 35.

sixty million tons a year. At the present rate of
mining, this would last about a century but Table V
shows that there has been an extremely rapid increase
in the rate of extraction. Since 1907, however, this
tendency has been less marked and the better grades
of iron ore may, therefore, actually last for fifty to
seventy years yet. Then, the rich deposits will be
gone and we must turn to the necessarily more
expensive and laborious methods of getting iron from
low grade ores. Fortunately, these ores exist in large
quantities else the Age of Steel would seem hastening
to an untimely close. The Conservation Commission estimates indicate the existence of some
75,000,000,000 long tons of ore not now worth working.[1] This should supply our needs for several
centuries yet, but the cost of obtaining a ton of iron
from this ore will probably be several times the cost
of mining and extraction at the present time when
high grade ores are scooped up with steam shovels
from great beds almost on the surface.

With the growing use of electric current for light
and power, copper is becoming more and more essential to modern industry. As shown in Table V, the
output has increased until, in 1912, it was nearly
eight hundred times as great as in 1850 and there is
every indication that this increase is to continue at a
rapid rate for many years to come. No estimates

[1] *Statistical Abstract of the United States for 1912*, p. 35.

are available as to the total supply of copper ore but the consensus of opinion seems to be that it is very large but mostly of a low grade and hence that the cost of mining and refining is destined to advance rather rapidly.[1]

Phosphate rock is a deposit of which the average citizen knows little but which, nevertheless, occupies a place of prime importance amongst our mineral resources. While phosphates are absolutely essential to the growth of grains, the supply of phosphorus in the soil is distinctly limited and is decreased by every grain crop grown. If, then, the fertility of the soil and present grain yields are to be maintained, the phosphorus must be replaced and this replacement must largely come from the deposits of calcium phosphate found in various sections of the country. The total store of rather high grade phosphate rock in the United States is estimated at about half a billion long tons.[2] At the rate of mining indicated by Table V for 1912, the supply will only last for a little over a century and a half and the rate of extraction is rising very rapidly. Fortunately, there are large deposits of low grade rock which may be utilized, but at a higher cost per ton of phosphoric oxide obtained.

In the sixties, a new fuel in the shape of petroleum

[1] Van Hise, Charles R., *The Conservation of Natural Resources*, pp. 74–79.

[2] Van Hise, Charles R., *The Conservation of Natural Resources*, pp. 320–334.

was discovered and, since that date, its production has increased by leaps and bounds. It is estimated that some 13,000,000,000 barrels of 42 gallons each are still to be pumped from the ground.[1] Over 200,000,000 barrels were drawn from the earth in 1912. Unless geologists are greatly mistaken, production will become much more difficult in the near future and rising prices will lessen the demands. At the present rate of use, some sixty years would probably see the supply in the United States exhausted. This is illustrated by the fact that, in the Appalachian field, the daily production per well has fallen from 207 barrels in the early days to less than two barrels at the present time.[2] At best, this variety of our natural resources is being depleted with great rapidity and seems destined, ere many decades, to practically disappear. Yet, despite countless warnings, we still recklessly squander this priceless heritage for uses in which a barrel possesses but relatively slight utility. We construct great locomotives and ships, to burn it in ever increasing quantities even though its superiority over coal is but slight and the fraction of its total energy utilized is but trivial; we even sprinkle it over our streets and highways, all regardless of the fact that, in so doing, we

[1] Van Hise, Charles R., *The Conservation of Natural Resources*, p. 47.

[2] Van Hise, Charles R., *The Conservation of Natural Resources*, p. 48.

are dissipating the material needed to light the lamps of the poor and propel the aeroplanes of the rich only a generation or two hence.

What has just been said of petroleum has still greater force when applied to natural gas. According to the best estimates,[1] most of the gas fields worth while will have been exhausted in the next score of· years and the use of natural gas in large quantities will become historical except in the occasional instances of new discoveries. Dr. Day also estimates that half of the gas drawn from the earth has been wasted or served but trivial uses. This valuable kind of natural wealth, then, must, likewise, soon be dropped from our inventory.

The minerals cited are typical of mineral resources in general. In every case, the extraction is becoming more and more rapid and the existing stock less and less abundant. Some of these minerals will last for decades, others for many centuries, but this does not alter the fact that, with the diminishing supply, they will all become harder and harder to obtain. Population grows apace, and hence, the per capita stock diminishes much more rapidly than does the total supply, but this abstract truth will not, in most cases, be vividly realized by the next few generations. The fact that will come home to them will be that a day's labor will tend gradually to

[1] Day, David T., *Natural Gas Resources of the United States*, Volume III, pp. 465–475.

procure less coal, less iron-ware, less copper wire,
and less gasoline than was formerly the case. For
this fact, many reasons will be ascribed besides the
true one of the using up of our natural wealth. Monopolies will be denounced and regulated; the party
in power will be turned out of office in disgrace; but
the minerals will still rise in value The rising cost
will be delayed by new discoveries, which will make
mining easier and transportation and refining less
difficult, but the more rapid looting of Nature's
storehouses, made possible by these new processes,
will only accentuate the steepness of the rising cost
curve at a later date, decades or centuries hence.

SUMMARY

The whole question of land supply may be summed
up as follows: Is the average American of to-day as
richly endowed with the gifts of nature as was the
average American of a century ago? To this question, the reply must be an emphatic "No!" The
city man has more crowded residence quarters; our
supply of farm land has not quite kept pace with
our population; our ranges have diminished greatly
in absolute area, and, to a much greater extent, when
considered relatively to population; our hunting
grounds have all but disappeared;[1] our forest area

[1] Something has already been done and much more may be
accomplished in the way of game-protection—especially in connection with the State and National forest reserves.

per capita has become insignificant as compared to that possessed by the Americans of a century since; and our mineral resources are diminishing steadily and surely. But social wealth consists not of land only but also of capital and consumers' goods. We shall next consider the supply of capital on hand at the various census years since 1850.

THE SUPPLY OF CAPITAL

Production ordinarily requires the co-operation of three forces, labor, capital, and productive natural resources. We have seen that each person, on the average, is, as time passes, becoming more and more poorly equipped with natural resources. If, however, he has better tools and machines, better means of transportation, better means of generating power, in other words more capital, he may still, even with poorer natural resources, gain a larger income. It is necessary, therefore, to see whether an increase in the capital supply per man has tended to offset the growing scarcity of the gifts of nature.

Unfortunately, the statistics of value of capital goods at the various census years are neither complete nor comparable. The term capital has been used to cover such things as amount invested, value of securities outstanding, value of land, and value of those objects known to the economist as social capital. Social capital, in the strict sense, includes only products of past industry and only such of those products as are used in the further production of wealth. Since we are, at this point, inquiring into the equipment of society, we shall attempt to separate out and consider only the active part of social capital, the machines, buildings, tools, railroads, trains, vessels, live stock, etc., which assist in the creation of new wealth—and omit those passive objects such as stocks of goods on the merchants' shelves, manufactured articles ready for distribution, grain on hand, etc., since these are transitory in their nature and have relatively little significance in showing the comparative degree to which man has equipped himself to overcome the difficulties of extracting a living from the earth.

In Table VI, we have an attempt to collect the various figures of the United States Census and combine them into a harmonious whole. While the numbers are, in no case, exact, it is believed that the errors are too small to vitiate any of the following conclusions. We see that the total supply of active capital has enormously increased, in fact that, in 1910, the value was about seventeen times as great as in 1850. In this great increase, all industries have participated but the fishing equipment has grown most slowly and the transportation facilities fastest of all. At no census year, has there been a recession in a single industry—development has been continuous in all lines.

But an increase in the total value of active capital

is not, in itself, significant. It must be compared
with the increase in population and with a changing

TABLE VI

		Business Buildings and Fixed Improvements.[1]	Railroads and Other Public Utilities.[2]	Movable Machinery, Tools, and Implements.[4]	Live Stock.[3]	Fisheries.[4]
THE ESTIMATED VALUE OF THE SUPPLY OF ACTIVE CAPITAL IN THE CONTINENTAL UNITED STATES IN MILLIONS OF DOLLARS.						
Census Year.	Total.[5]					
1850	2,757	1,113	639	399	599	7
1860	5,900	2,160	1,868	665	1,198	9
1870	8,978	2,975	3,109	1,206	1,678	10
1880	13,636	4,117	5,386	2,373	1,735	25
1890	19,298	5,700	8,366	2,665	2,538	29
1900	24,783	7,250	10,926	4,006	3,197	34
1910	47,961	13,301	23,319	5,995	5,296	50

price-level before we can arrive at any conclusions
concerning the influence of the change upon the social
welfare. The third column in Table VII indicates
that the per capita value of active capital has steadily
grown larger until, in 1910, it has become more than
four times as great as in 1850. Only in the Civil
War period has this apparent increase been due
wholly to changing prices for, if the per capita value

[1] See Table VIa, Appendix.
[2] See Table VIb, Appendix.
[3] Estimated from United States Census figures.
[4] See Table VIc, Appendix.
[5] Error probably not greater than 25 per cent. Figures for
1900 and 1910 more accurate than the others.

is divided by the price index, we obtain an index of
amount which climbs upward until the **quantity** per
capita existing in 1850 is more than quadrupled.

TABLE VII

Census Year.	Total Value of the Active Capital Supply in Millions of Dollars.[1]	Per Capita Value of Active Capital. v	Price Index.[2] p	Index of Quantity of Capital Per Capita. $\frac{v}{p}$
	QUANTITY OF ACTIVE CAPITAL IN THE UNITED STATES (outlying possessions excluded).			
1850	2,757	$119	139.2	85
1860	5,900	188	141.3	133
1870	8,978	233	221.6	105
1880	13,636	272	132.4	205
1890	19,298	307	113.6	270
1900	24,783	326	101.7	321
1910	47,961	521	126.5	412

The only backward step shown is in the decade 1860
to 1870 and this was due, probably, to the wholesale
destruction of capital by the Civil War, a blow from
which the Southern States had only begun to recover
in 1870.   The more or less chaotic conditions of the
South in 1870 may also have resulted in some incompleteness in the Census returns.

The term, "amount of active capital per capita,"
may need some explanation.   In this case, we evi-

[1] See Table VI.

[2] Wholesale prices—United States Bureau of Labor index;
Base 1890–1899; for year preceding the Census in each case.
Bulletin 114, United States Bureau of Labor Statistics, p. 149.

dently are not measuring capital in units of weight
or volume. In every practical sense, the amount of
capital is increased when a ton of iron ore and two

FIGURE 3

QUANTITY AND MONEY VALUE PER CAPITA OF ACTIVE CAPITAL
AND CONSUMPTION GOODS IN THE UNITED STATES [1]

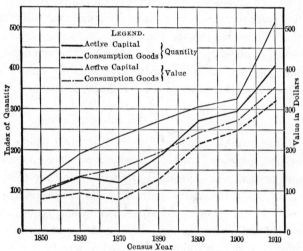

tons of coal are converted into half a ton of steel
rails. Amount in this sense is, therefore, related
somewhat to the Marxian idea of units of labor cost
or, on the other hand, to units of productive power.
On the whole, the index numbers representing either
of these latter ideas would probably be quite similar.

[1] See tables VII and VIII.

We may safely conclude, therefore, that the equipment of the average American of to-day for wresting the treasures from the grasp of Nature is far superior to the equipment possessed by the men who fought the Civil War and that tools, machines, and improvements are constantly becoming more and more complex and efficient.   As natural resources have become more scanty, the means for collecting and utilizing them have constantly improved.   Has the gain in one case offset the loss in the other?   The amount of the product should partly answer this question. This will be taken up in a later chapter.

THE SUPPLY OF CONSUMPTION GOODS

Most capital and land are of little direct utility to human beings.   It is their products which are sought and prized.   The ultimate products which are ready to be used to satisfy human wants are known as consumption goods.   Many consumption goods are capable of only one use, hence, are used up with relative rapidity while other articles may be utilized by successive generations.   Thus, food and fuel rapidly disappear while houses and carriages last for a number of years.   Human happiness depends to a very considerable extent upon the supply of consumption goods but, in the case of the less durable goods, the stock on hand at a given time is of little moment.   The frontier settler often lays in flour for a year when he goes to mill—the modern city housewife buys bread for only one day and other food in similar proportions, yet the city family may have a better food supply than the settler on the edge of civilization. In the case of perishable consumption goods, therefore, it is not the existing stock but the daily supply that is of consequence.

When, however, we deal with durable consumption goods, the stock on hand becomes of prime importance. We desire large and luxurious houses and motor cars, many articles of furniture, a variety of jewelry and clothing and, in order that each person may possess such an assortment of commodities, society must accumulate a large stock of the articles in question. When we speak of a city or nation being rich or opulent, we usually think of beautiful dwellings, splendid churches and elaborate public buildings, all equipped with elegant furnishings. It is in these things that communities and individuals take pride— hence the stock of durable consumption goods is, in many ways, a good criterion of the social welfare.

Unfortunately, our statistics of the value of consumption goods on hand at the various census periods are little more than rough guesses, yet, crude as they are, they apparently point with certainty to a rapid rise in the total stock of this kind of wealth.

Table VIII indicates that, just as in the case of active capital, consumption goods have increased in

value per capita to some four times the amount on
hand in 1850 and, when the value is divided by the
price index, we see that an even greater increase has

TABLE VIII

THE ESTIMATED VALUE AND QUANTITY OF CONSUMPTION GOODS IN THE UNITED STATES (outlying possessions excluded).				
Census Year.	Total Value in Millions of Dollars.[1]	Value per Capita.[3] v	Price Index.[2] p	Relative Quantity of Consumption Goods per Capita. $\frac{v}{p}$
1850	2,317	$100	139.2	72
1860	4,197	133	141.3	94
1870	5,968	155	221.6	70
1880	9,645	192	132.4	145
1890	15,239	242	113.6	213
1900	20,824	274	101.7	269
1910	32,976	359	126.5	284

taken place. The same backset due to the Civil
War is very marked and, likewise, the remarkable
expansion in the decade 1870 to 1880, when industry
was profiting by new inventions and the richest
part of the Mississippi Valley was just being fairly
opened up. Evidently, the popular impression is

[1] See Table VIIIa, Appendix.

[2] United States Bureau of Labor index of wholesale prices; not
well adapted but the best available; *Bulletin 114, United States
Bureau of Labor Statistics*, p. 149.

[3] Roughly estimated—error in last three decades perhaps 15
per cent, in earlier decades as high as 30 per cent.

true that, as far as dwellings, furnishings, vehicles, clothing, etc., are concerned, we live in a state of luxury that our fathers knew not of. Thus, we are at least partially recompensed and perhaps far more than repaid for the loss of many of the pleasures connected with the free use of field and forest.

CHAPTER IV

THE DISTRIBUTION OF WEALTH AMONG FAMILIES

WHAT DISTRIBUTION OF WEALTH IS BEST?

IN the preceding chapter, the fact was brought out that the total and average supply of capital and consumers' goods available for the inhabitants of the United States has been increasing at a rapid rate. While this fact would be admitted by most observers, many writers contend that the increase or decrease of the per capita wealth is a matter of no particular significance. They attach primary importance not to totals or averages but to questions of distribution. They point out that it is perfectly possible for the average wealth to show a large increase and, at the same time, for the great mass of the people to descend into more and more straitened circumstances. The average wealth would be greatly increased by the addition of a few dozen billionaires to our population but this might give little more shelter to the homeless or food to the hungry.

Some of these writers go further than the placing of a merely hypothetical question in the field for discussion and contend that the past half century has been an era in which all gains have been absorbed by a few plutocrats while the great masses of the population have become poorer and poorer. Such arguments can only be verified or disproved by a direct study of the facts, and facts of this nature are necessarily statistical. In the following pages, the attempt will be made to throw some degree of light upon the matter.

But, of what importance, after all, is the whole question of the distribution of **wealth** among families? Is not the really fundamental thing the proper distribution of **income**? These two ideas are too frequently discussed as if they were practically synonomous and, yet, there is no necessary dependence of one upon the other.

Imagine, for example, a state in which all the productive wealth is the personal property of the sovereign. He holds title to every mine and factory; all the flocks and herds are his, alone. But he is a benign ruler and offers employment to all in well regulated factories or mines, splendidly equipped public utilities, or on model farms. Further, these industries are so productive that he can and does pay good wages and salaries. His administration shows no favoritism but deals with each according to his merits. In times of sickness, death or disaster, he relieves the wants of the unfortunate and ministers to their needs. No other nation can compare with his dominions in general prosperity; no other people are so happy and contented; and, yet, no one but the king owns an acre of land or a dollar's worth of capital. All the productive wealth of the nation is concentrated in his hands. Nevertheless, the distribution of income has been reduced to an ideal basis. Under such circumstances, a demand that the people own the wealth of the land would appear to be sheer folly—an evidence of the chronic dissatisfaction of some unbalanced agitator or blatant demagogue.

This picture would have seemed less impossible to idealists of the eighteenth century than to Americans of to-day but does it differ so much, after all, from the ideal state, pictured by some Socialist writers of recent years? True, they would substitute a beneficent democratic government for the benign monarch; but the income is dispensed with the same unerring wisdom and fairness; and, likewise, the result portrayed is universal prosperity and happiness.

But we need not dream either of the monarch who is all-wise and ever-just or of the same perfection embodied in a socialistic regime in order to conceive of a state with a system of wealth distribution possessing many of the characteristics of that existing under the conditions cited above. We need only to imagine the fortunes of some of the great magnates of the present day to go on increasing for another century at the same rate as during the last thirty years to find the wealth of the country all concentrated in a few hands. Suppose that their heirs should establish an oligarchy just as kind and benevolent and fair as the government of the ruler of the Utopian kingdom. All the people might still be prosperous and contented and, yet, they would hold title to no wealth of consequence.

We perceive, therefore, that equality in wealth distribution is no necessary accompaniment of equality of income or of general well-being. Why is it, then, that economists have laid such stress on the question of wealth ownership? The answer is that the possession of wealth gives power. Whoever controls the property of a nation becomes thereby the virtual ruler thereof. And we do not possess faith enough in the inherent wisdom, virtue, justice, and benevolence of those possessing great wealth to feel confident that they will unselfishly and wisely use the power obtained entirely, or even largely in the interests of the common weal. Did we possess such faith, we could view with perfect equanimity the concentration of all the wealth of the nation in the hands of one, or of a dozen citizens. Since this form of confidence is strikingly lacking, there is a strong demand among many non-socialists that wealth, and hence power, be widely distributed. As to just how wide an area should be covered by this distribution, few will agree. Some would be satisfied to have a select class of the most capable citizens own the bulk of the property—others believe in a distribution approaching equality. Between these extremes might be found an indefinite number of gradations.

If we presuppose the existence of a legal and economic system of a competitive nature, such as that with which we are most familiar, we find that there are four fundamental reasons why it is desirable that wealth should be in the hands of the many rather than of the few. These may be enumerated as follows:

1. Under existing conditions, the state does not guarantee a sufficient degree of assistance in case of misfortune to prevent want and misery. It only steps in to prevent starvation or to relieve acute distress. Under all ordinary circumstances, the individual is expected to help himself and recourse to the state for aid, generally means that the applicant feels himself disgraced and is branded as a pauper by the community.[1] This being true, it becomes

[1] It is undoubtedly true that, at the present time, by workmen's compensation, old age pensions, free medical treatment, etc., the state is tending more and more to obviate the pressing necessity for wealth accumulation in the hands of the poorest class. While these measures are doing much and probably will do more to alleviate acute distress due to misfortune, there is no present prospect that governmental aid will, in the near future, take the place of family savings in furnishing real comfort and security in times of stress.

imperative that every self-respecting citizen provide for himself protection against disaster and the best form of such protection is accumulated wealth. In time of unemployment or sickness or bereavement, there is a most striking dissimilarity between the circumstances of the man with a few thousand dollars worth of property and those of his neighbor who has had the same income in the past but has laid away nothing for the "rainy day." One is ready, when the shock is over, to take his accustomed place again in the army of industry. The other has been forced to a dependence upon charity, has thereby sacrificed a degree of his manhood and self-respect, and will probably never again be as good a member of society as before. This being the case, it is certainly desirable, under a competitive system of society, that as large a percentage of the population as possible be equipped with this safeguard of wealth—for the man does not live who is sure of escaping the ills and accidents that befall the human race.

2. Another advantage of wealth, akin to that just cited, is that it gives to the possessor a much greater freedom of movement, a wider sphere of action, than is otherwise vouchsafed to him. Without wealth, one is seldom in a position to bargain well as to wages or salary. One **must** find a position and so the first offer must be accepted. One cannot travel from place to place in search of better opportunities—for travel

costs money. As a result, freedom of competition is restricted,[1] the job and the man do not get together, and the number of "square pegs in round holes", with all the attendant unhappiness, is bound to be materially increased.

3. Another useful phase of widely distributed ownership of wealth is that it makes for social stability. The propertied man is seldom an enemy of law and order. He does not favor revolution for he has something to lose. True, he may be too conservative, but history does not show that those nations have advanced most in which revolution has been frequent. The nations most free from internal strife and bloodshed are those in which a large fraction of the people have possessed some considerable property and have been able, by their leadership, to maintain law and order. And, while there may be dispute as to whether this is or is not the fundamental cause, it can scarcely be denied that the nations which have contributed most to the world progress of the last four hundred years have been those in which there existed a strong and virile middle class to whom anarchy and lawlessness were anathema. On the

[1] Many writers have made much of the fact that the ownership of real estate hampers the movement of workingmen with families. While this is true, to a degree, its importance has probably been exaggerated for it apparently applies mainly to those particular cases in which there is no local competition by employers for the services of the worker and, even in such instances, real property is, ordinarily, not difficult to lease.

other hand, whether we turn to those oriental despotisms or to certain Spanish-American republics,
which have alike been dominated by rich and powerful grandees supported by the toil of a half-beggared
populace, we find never-ending cycles of riot and
revolution and observe them to-day as nations politi-
cally and morally a century behind the times.

4. The fourth great advantage of widely distributed wealth is dynamic rather than static in its
nature. This depends not only upon the fact that
many people now **possess** wealth but also upon the
fact that they **acquired** this property by their own
efforts. If many people were well-to-do but if all
had inherited their wealth, the propertyless young
man would then feel it a perfectly futile task to
attempt to acquire a competence. No one in the
vicinity having succeeded in so doing, it would
evidently be a waste of energy to try. But, on the
other hand, if the older men of his acquaintance have
attained affluence through hard work or use of their
native talents, the young man feels that he can do
likewise. Wealth means power and ease and luxury
and display. These lure him on to strenuous endeavor and cause him to toil early and late in the
pursuit of riches. And it is this strenuous endeavor
of the millions that amasses the capital, that searches
out the new inventions and discoveries, that does all
those things which spell economic progress.

No other stimulus to labor and efficiency has ever been more powerful than this desire for riches. Mere hope of current income is a much less powerful incentive to action. The day laborer works harder because he hopes to lay aside something for a rainy day and for old age. The clerk and the mechanic put in a little extra time, save a little more, in order that they may own their homes and educate their children. The business man devotes more energy to his affairs in order that he may build the dreamed of mansion or win a name as a captain of industry. And it is this extra effort, this saving of the dollars accomplished through self-denial, that accumulates the masses of capital—the tools, the machines, the ships, the railways, the buildings—essential to modern methods of industry. Were the productivity of the great masses of the people to be slackened ever so little, their savings would probably decrease in much greater proportion for it is usually only the surplus above bare necessities that is, in part, saved. The savings of the few rich would, alone, be entirely inadequate to supply the capital for the new enterprises required to produce the necessities of life for our growing population and, without the accumulations of the common people, we should witness a retrogression in industry, wealth, and prosperity. Unless, then, other untried means can be shown to serve equally well as incentives to production, the

possibility of accumulating wealth must be regarded
as one of the mainstays of our economic civilization.
But, it must be kept in mind that, if we are to depend
upon the possibility of accumulating wealth as a spur
to the activity of mankind, this possibility must not
be merely the rare chance in a lottery. To a certain
type of mind, the millionth chance to obtain a great
fortune may prove very alluring, but, to the large
mass of conservative people, such opportunities
appear too remote to lead to any sustained effort.
To the majority, a reasonable prospect that hard
work and self-denial will bring a competence for old
age or an opportunity for leisure and pleasure is
necessary in order to materially affect their activity
as producers and savers. We can draw conclusions
concerning the future only by a study of past and
present conditions. If it is known that a large fraction of the people actually do succeed in gathering
together enough property to be worth while, the
effort to imitate them will continue but, if the great
majority, despite their striving to get ahead, die in
poverty—then effort is sure to slacken materially
with a corresponding loss in productivity and a great
decrease in savings. One of the principal reasons
for the poverty of the masses and the absence of any
considerable middle class in the Oriental despotisms
is that any considerable accumulation of wealth by a
common citizen has always been a signal for plunder

by the tax gatherers. As a result, little capital has been accumulated and industrial progress has been rendered next to impossible.

We have enumerated four fundamental advantages of having a large share of the population participate in the ownership of wealth. Are we to conclude, then, that a practically equal division of wealth is most desirable for a democracy? Some persons would adhere to this view but more would advocate a moderate degree of inequality roughly proportional to the general ability of the citizens. By the term **general** ability, we cannot mean ability to acquire wealth under existing conditions, else we beg the whole question. We must refer only to those differences in skill which would be manifested in most branches of activity. It is easy to find a man in almost any line of employment who is **twice** as efficient as another employee but it is very rare to find one who is **ten times** as efficient. It is common, however, to see one man possessing not **ten** times but **a thousand** times the wealth of his neighbor. This discrepancy represents ability of only one type—the faculty of taking advantage of existing laws and circumstances to acquire property rights—and these rights are too frequently obtained by flagrant violations of the spirit if not the letter of the law. It must also be admitted that wealth tends to breed wealth—that it is relatively much easier for the rich man to

cause his small fortune to grow into a large one than
for the poor man to accumulate a small fortune.

Is there, then, any social advantage in allowing
men who have been fortunate enough to be born rich
or who have the one remarkably developed faculty
of being able to amass wealth by legal or illegal,
honorable or dishonorable means to collect or retain
control of tremendous masses of capital and land,
drawing annually economic revenue therefrom? Is
this more desirable, socially, than to transfer the
wealth of the world for safe-keeping to the musical
genius, the lightning calculator, or some other person
having a remarkable development of some one natural
gift?

From the standpoint of merit, one of these prodigies
is exactly as much entitled to be a Croesus as the
other. The only possible excuses, then, for allowing
the great money-getter to retain his vast gains are
that society is too lethargic to make the necessary
effort to deprive the holder of his money or that, in
some way, society will be benefitted by allowing the
fortune to remain in his hands. The defender of the
millionaire, of course, bases his arguments upon the
latter contention. We are all familiar with the
reasons cited centuries ago for the maintenance of a
leisure class—the desirability of fostering art, culture,
etc. These are now so much more widely diffused
than in the older days that arguments of this nature

have lost most of their force. About the only serious reason which can now be advanced in favor of wealth concentration is that it is necessary in order to secure a maximum national dividend—that exceptional rewards to the captains of industry result in exceptionally efficient production, thus increasing greatly the incomes of the people as a whole. This belief is not necessarily based on the untenable hypothesis that enormous rewards are necessary in order to secure the requisite high degree of exertion and endeavor but rather it is contended that, if there were no millionaires, modern large-scale industry would hardly be possible—that corporations without leading stockholders in control would, at best, be weak, vacillating and inefficient, and that the fifty millions which we permit the industrial captain to accumulate have been the price of an added production of one hundred million or two hundred million dollars' worth of goods which society would never have possessed had not the efficient control been paid for at a tremendous price. This is not the same as saying that we must pay the great organizer so exorbitantly for his efforts. It merely presupposes a necessity for a great accumulation of funds in the hands of one man in order to attain maximum productivity. The great entrepreneur is made a trustee for society.

The opponents of this theory would cite the fact that many of the very wealthy are not great entrepreneurs and do little by their efforts or by their wealth to further efficient production. They would also contend that it has not been conclusively proved that a corporation with many small stockholders might not be an extremely effective working organization, though it must be admitted that most large coöperative concerns have not been extremely successful. As a matter of fact, it seems to be true that the connection between concentrated wealth and efficient large scale enterprise is, as yet, not clearly understood. If industry is to continue under the régime of private property, it seems desirable either to prove the dependence of successful large scale production upon the concentration of wealth—thus justifying this concentration—or else to admit that our laws and institutions should be so reconstructed as to maintain that type of distribution deemed socially most desirable.

We have now considered the abstract arguments for and against a wide and relatively uniform distribution of wealth. We are all well aware that the division of riches in the United States is far from being on a basis of equality. As to just how far removed from equality it actually is, there has been little unanimity of opinion and accurate information is scanty and little known. For centuries, America has been known as "The Land of Opportunity." To the poverty stricken European laborer, it is a

country in which a few years suffice to convert a
pauper into a prince. On the other hand, to many
hard working Americans, the chances for affluence
have appeared to be surprisingly few. The question
as to which view is correct can only be settled by
statistical inquiry and, as yet, but few investigations
have been made which throw light upon the subject.

THE EXISTING DISTRIBUTION OF WEALTH

But, we are interested not only in the present distribution of property but in the changes that have
taken place therein. ✳Are the rich getting ever richer
and the poor always more poverty stricken? Are
the domains of the millionaires continually encroaching more and more upon the modest holdings of the
middle class or upon the petty properties of the poor?
Is the middle class doomed to extinction and shall we
soon find the handful of plutocrats, the modern barons
of wealth, lined up squarely in opposition to the
propertyless masses with no buffer between to lessen
the chances of open battle? With the middle class
gone and the laborer condemned to remain a lifelong
wage-earner with no hope of attaining wealth or even
a competence in his old age, all the conditions are
ripe for a crowning class-conflict equalling in intensity
and bitterness anything pictured by the most radical
follower of Karl Marx. Is this condition soon coming
to pass? We can only judge the future by the past

and to judge intelligently we must again cast aside all preconceptions and prejudices and turn to unbiased statistical evidence for our answer. As before stated, this variety of information is meager in amount but that which does exist throws some very interesting light upon the questions which we are seeking to solve. We shall consider the results of the two investigations whose records are at hand.

The principal, and best known, source of information is the *Twenty-fifth Annual Report of the Massachusetts Bureau of Labor.* This Bureau made a careful study of the value of estates probated in Massachusetts during four different three year periods, viz. 1829–1831, 1859–1861, 1879–1881, and 1889–1891, the years in each case being inclusive. The results appear on pages 265–267 of their report.

In many ways, Massachusetts is a state very well adapted to show the changing tendencies of wealth distribution in the United States. It is primarily industrial in nature and, if property is being concentrated in a few hands, it would seem more likely to be the case in an industrial than in an agricultural state. Furthermore, Massachusetts possesses many cities, one being a great metropolis, and concentration is generally thought to appear far more strikingly in the city than in the rural regions. Yet, Boston is not, like New York, the financial headquarters of

6

the nation and so would be less likely to represent a tendency abnormal to the country as a whole.

The Massachusetts statistics possess the decided merit of having all estates classified as to ownership by males or females. On the other hand, the chief defect which causes difficulty in obtaining an accurate picture of the distribution of estates at each period is that, in some forty per cent of the cases, no inventory was filed and, hence, the size of the estates is unknown. In the opinion of the original investigators, the non-inventoried estates were probably somewhat larger than those for which inventories appear.[1] For the purposes of computation, we shall do the only feasible thing and assume that the size and distribution of non-inventoried estates did not differ materially from the corresponding figures for those estates for which inventories were filed. A comparison with the mortality figures in Massachusetts shows that, in each period, the number of deaths of males over twenty-five years of age greatly exceeded the number of estates probated. The obvious conclusion is that, in most of the instances not probated, the property was insignificant in value. We shall assume that five hundred dollars' worth was the upper limit with an average amount of $375 in the first period and $400 in each of the two latter periods.

[1] *Twenty-fifth Annual Report of the Massachusetts Bureau of Labor*, p. 66.

With these assumptions, we may proceed to estimate the distribution of wealth among men in Massachusetts at death. This, if accurate, will be a fair picture of the value of property actually accumulated during a lifetime and will enable us to get some idea of the hope of accumulation inspired at each of the given periods by the surroundings of the average man—by the actual success of his neighbors. It will also enable us to see, even more accurately than could the man at the time, the real chances for financial success.

We must remember, however, that statistics of the estates of male decedents will not serve to show the exact distribution of wealth among those persons living. In every instance, the **average** family wealth is greater than is indicated by the studies of the size of estates of men, for the family wealth consists of the possessions of both husband and wife and, in many cases, the latter owns very considerable property in her own name.

This underestimate of the family wealth is perhaps more than offset by the fact that, in a country like the United States, the average man is probably richer at the close of his life than during his younger years. This latter fact does not, however, impair the usefulness of the figures for the purpose in hand, for the young man is likely to be far more inspired to endeavor by the knowledge that the well-to-do

TABLE IX

	The Estimated Distribution of Estates of Men Dying in Massachusetts [3]					
Period.	Value of Estate in Thousands of Dollars.	Number of Estates in Class.	Percentage of Total Number of Estates.	Total Value of Estates in Class in Thousands of Dollars.	Percentage of Total Value of Estates.	Average Value of Estates in Class
	Total	15,285[1]	100.000	55,071	100.000	$ 3,603
	Under 0.5	10,794	70.620	4,048	7.350	375
	0.5 but under 1	686	4.488	604	1.097	880
1859	1 " " 5	2,279	14.911	6,153	11.172	2,700
	5 " " 10	735	4.808	5,218	9.475	7,100
to	10 " " 25	466	3.048	7,316	13.284	15,700
	25 " " 50	151	.987	5,345	9.705	35,400
1861	50 " " 100	90	.588	6,228	11.310	69,200
	100 " " 200	50	.327	6,535	11.868	130,700
	200 " " 300	19	124	4,551	8.263	239,500
	300 " " 400	5	.033	1,717	3.118	343,500
	400 " " 500	3	.020	1,425	2.588	475,000
	500 and over	7	.046	5,931	10 770	848,700
	Total	28,086[2]	100 000	137,837	100.000	$ 4,907
	Under 0.5	21,361	76 058	8,544	6 199	400
	0.5 but under 1	865	3.079	839	609	970
1879	1 " " 5	3,114	11.087	8,564	6.213	2,750
	5 " " 10	1,152	4.101	8,410	6.101	7,300
to	10 " " 25	844	3 005	13,420	9.736	15,900
	25 " " 50	351	1.250	12,144	8.810	34,600
1881	50 " " 100	193	.687	13,412	9.730	69,500
	100 " " 200	103	.367	14,573	10.572	141,500
	200 " " 300	40	.142	9,560	6.935	239,200
	300 " " 400	21	.075	7,398	5.367	352,300
	400 " " 500	11	.039	4,829	3.503	439,000
	500 and over	31	.110	36,144	26.225	1,166,000

[1] Estimated from the *United States Census for 1860, Mortality and Miscellaneous Statistics*, p. 44

[2] Estimated from the *Twenty-eighth Annual Report of the Massachusetts State Board of Health*, pp. 744, 756

TABLE IX—*Continued*

Period.	Value of Estate in Thousands of Dollars.	Number of Estates in Class.	Percentage of Total Number of Estates.	Total Value of Estates in Class in Thousands of Dollars.	Percentage of Total Value of Estates.	Average Value of Estates in Class.
	THE ESTIMATED DISTRIBUTION OF ESTATES OF MEN DYING IN MASSACHUSETTS.					
	Total	35,148[4]	100.000	202.695	100.000	$ 5,767
	Under 0.5	23,151	65.864	9,260	4.568	400
	0.5 but under 1	1,466	4.172	1,378	.680	940
1889	1 " " 5	5,715	16.262	15,432	7.614	2,700
	5 " " 10	2,005	5.704	14,637	7.220	7,300
to	10 " " 25	1,612	4.586	25,791	12.725	16,000
	25 " " 50	537	1.528	18,901	9.324	35,200
1891	50 " " 100	334	.950	23,480	11.585	70,300
	100 " " 200	176	.501	24,148	11.913	137,200
	200 " " 300	59	.168	14,632	7.218	248,000
	300 " " 400	28	.080	9,492	4.683	339,000
	400 " " 500	18	.051	8,270	4.080	459,500
	500 and over	47	.134	37,274	18.390	793,000

men of his acquaintance have gained their property by their own efforts than he would be by seeing that he was poor while many other young men were rich. The latter comparison is likely to breed envy while the former gives rise to ambition.

Tables IX and X present the statistical facts of the case as they appear when adjustments have been

[3] Estimated, in general, from the *Twenty-fifth Annual Report of the Massachusetts Bureau of Statistics of Labor*, pp. 264–267.

[4] Estimated from the *United States Census for 1890, Vital and Social Statistics*, Part III, p. 186.

made according to the assumptions previously stated.

TABLE X

		ESTATES OF GIVEN VALUE.			
PERIOD.	VALUE OF ESTATE IN THOUSANDS OF DOLLARS.	Number.	Percentage of Total Number.	Value in Thousands of Dollars.	Percentage of Total Value.

CUMULATIVE[1] PERCENTAGES OF THE NUMBER AND VALUE OF ESTATES OF MEN DYING IN MASSACHUSETTS.[2]

PERIOD	VALUE OF ESTATE IN THOUSANDS OF DOLLARS	Number	Percentage of Total Number	Value in Thousands of Dollars	Percentage of Total Value
	Under 0.5	10,794	70.620	4,048	7.350
	" 1	11,480	75.108	4,652	8.447
	" 5	13,759	90.019	10,805	19.619
1859	" 10	14,494	94.827	16,023	29.094
	" 25	14,960	97.875	23,339	42.378
to	" 50	15,111	98.862	28,684	52.083
	" 100	15,201	99.450	34,912	63.393
1861	" 200	15,251	99.777	41,447·	75.261
	" 300	15,270	99.901	45,998	83.524
	" 400	15,275	99.934	47,715	86.642
	" 500	15,278	99.954	49,140	89.230
	All estates	15,285	100.000	55,071	100.000
	Under 0.5	21,361	76.058	8,544	6.199
	" 1	22,226	79.137	9,383	6.808
	" 5	25,340	90.224	17,947	13.021
1879	" 10	26,492	94.325	26,357	19.122
	" 25	27,336	97.330	39,777	28.858
to	" 50	27,687	98.550	51,921	37.668
	" 100	27,880	99.267	65,333	47.398
1881	" 200	27,983	99.634	79,906	57.970
	" 300	28,023	99.776	89,466	64.905
	" 400	28,044	99.851	96,864	70.272
	" 500	28,055	99.890	101,693	73.775
	All estates	28,086	100.000	137,837	100.000

[1] A number is cumulative when it includes all smaller quantities.

[2] Derived from Table IX.

TABLE X—*Continued*

		ESTATES OF GIVEN VALUE.			
PERIOD.	VALUE OF ESTATE IN THOUSANDS OF DOLLARS.	Number.	Percentage of Total Number.	Value in Thousands of Dollars.	Percentage of Total Value.
	Under 0.5	23,151	65.864	9,260	4.568
	" 1	26,617	70.036	10,638	5.248
	" 5	30,332	86.298	26,070	12.862
1889	" 10	32,337	92.002	40,707	20.082
	" 25	33,949	96.588	66,498	32.807
to	" 50	34,486	98.116	85,399	42.131
	" 100	34,820	99.066	108,879	53.716
1891	" 200	34,996	99.567	133,027	65.629
	" 300	35,055	99.735	147,659	72.847
	" 400	35,083	99.815	157,151	77.530
	" 500	35,101	99.866	165,421	81.610
	All estates	35,148	100.000	202,695	100.000

Title row of the table:

CUMULATIVE PERCENTAGES OF THE NUMBER AND VALUE OF ESTATES OF MEN DYING IN MASSACHUSETTS.

The tables show definitely the wide gulf existing between the average estate of the richest class and the average holding of the poorest men. They show the great numbers of the poor as compared to the little handful of the rich. But, by use of the curves devised for the purpose by Dr. Max O. Lorenz, now statistician of the Interstate Commerce Commission, it is much easier to portray clearly in our minds the relative distribution of wealth at different times and places. If the cumulative percentages of Table X are plotted against each other as shown in Figs. 4 and 5, the relative distribution at each period is

Figure 4

Relative Distribution of Wealth Among Decedents, Massachusetts and Wisconsin[1]

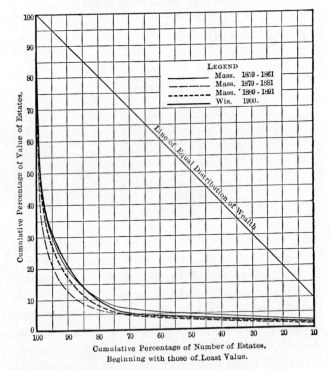

Cumulative Percentage of Value of Estates.

LEGEND
Mass. 1859 - 1861
Mass. 1879 - 1881
Mass. 1889 - 1891
Wis. 1900.

Line of Equal Distribution of Wealth

Cumulative Percentage of Number of Estates,
Beginning with those of Least Value.

indicated by the positions of the curves. If each family were equally wealthy, evidently one fourth of the population would possess one fourth of the

[1] See Tables IX and X.

wealth, one half of the population one half of the
wealth, and so on, and the resulting graph would be
a straight line at an angle of forty-five degrees, as
shown in the illustration. The more that the curves
actually bow away from this line the more unequally
is wealth distributed. The curves in Fig. 4 are bent
so very far away from this line of equal distribution
that they indicate an extremely uneven apportionment of goods.

Fig. 5 is merely a reproduction of the upper segment of the Lorenz curves shown in Fig. 4 but the
horizontal scale has been so enlarged as to separate
the graphs. This enables one to study the distribution among the very rich, which the relatively
small horizontal deflection renders impossible in
Fig. 4. A striking thing about this illustration is
that there is so little discrepancy between the different
periods for Massachusetts. Wealth became most
unevenly divided about 1880 and, since that time,
there has been a slight tendency toward greater
equality of possessions. But no one could seriously
contend that the figures show any startling change.
The general distribution was not greatly different in
1890 from what it was in the days immediately
preceding the Civil War despite the fact that between
the two dates there was a striking growth of large
scale production. During these thirty years, the
volume of wealth had increased much faster than

had the population, but "the few" continuously possessed the lion's share and "the many" had almost nothing, no matter which of the three periods is taken into consideration.

FIGURE 5

RELATIVE DISTRIBUTION OF ESTATES OF WEALTHY DECEDENTS, MASSACHUSETTS AND WISCONSIN[1]

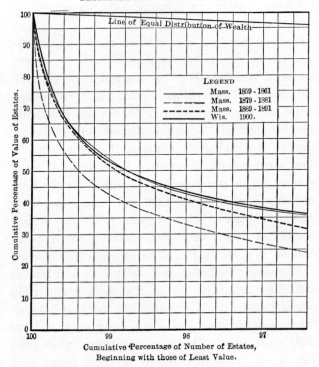

LEGEND

Mass.   1859 - 1861
Mass.   1879 - 1881
Mass.   1889 - 1891
Wis.   1900.

Cumulative Percentage of Number of Estates, Beginning with those of Least Value.

[1] See Tables IX and X.

Before going into greater detail, it may be well to compare the general distribution of an Eastern State like Massachusetts with that in the six counties of Dane, Grant, Manitowoc, Milwaukee, Racine, and Winnebago in the Mississippi Valley State of Wisconsin. These counties, while containing much fertile farm land, can scarcely be held to be typical of the agricultural regions of the United States for they include one large city, Milwaukee, and three others of over 25,000 inhabitants. The concentration of population in the cities of these counties is such as to make them fairly comparable in their characteristics to the State of Massachusetts. The Wisconsin investigation covers the distribution of estates during the year 1900 in the six counties mentioned. The results were compiled in manuscript form by Dr. Max Lorenz. Since this inquiry follows, by about a decade, the last of the Massachusetts studies it might be considered as a possible indicator of any notable changes occurring near the close of the last century. At any rate, it is interesting to compare these figures with those worked out for Massachusetts in order to detect marked similarities or differences between the two.

Fortunately, as in the case of Massachusetts, the estates of males were differentiated from those of females. It has been assumed, likewise, that those dying under twenty-five years of age who had estates

worth probating were a negligible fraction of the
population and that the estates not probated were
included in the list of those valued at less than five
hundred dollars. The total deaths of males over
twenty-five years of age was approximated from the
figures shown in the United States Census of Vital
Statistics, these figures probably being as accurate as
any available.

TABLE XI

THE ESTIMATED[1] DISTRIBUTION, ACCORDING TO VALUE, OF THE
ESTATES OF ALL MEN OVER TWENTY-FIVE YEARS OF AGE
DYING IN THE COUNTIES OF DANE, GRANT, MANITOWOC
MILWAUKEE, RACINE, AND WINNEBAGO IN THE STATE OF
WISCONSIN IN THE YEAR 1900.

Value of Estate in Thousands of Dollars.	Number of Estates in Class.	Percentage of Total Number of Estates.	Total Value of Estates in Class in Thousands of Dollars.	Percentage of Total Value of Estates.	Average Value of Estates in Class.
Total	2,332	100.000	11,105	100.000	$ 4,762
Under .5	1,570	67.323	589	5.304	375
.5 but under 1.0	74	3.174	53	.477	716
1.0 " " 2.5	165	7.076	286	2.575	1,733
2.5 " " 5.0	161	6.904	633	5.700	3,931
5.0 " " 7.5	108	4.631	607	5.466	5,620
7.5 " " 10.0	75	3.216	617	5.556	8,226
10.0 " " 15.0	66	2.830	788	7.096	11,940
15.0 " " 25.0	50	2.144	845	7.609	16,900
25.0 " " 50.0	33	1.415	1,116	10.051	33,812
50.0 " " 100.0	12	.515	835	7.519	69,583
100.0 " " 500.0	16	.686	3,492	31.445	218,220
500.0 and over	2	.086	1,244	11.202	622,000

[1] Estimated from the *United States Census on Vital Statistics
for 1900* and the manuscript study by Max Lorenz on *The
Distribution of Wealth in Six Wisconsin Counties.*

TABLE XII

CUMULATIVE[2] PERCENTAGES OF THE NUMBER AND VALUE OF ESTATES OF MEN DYING IN THE YEAR 1900 IN SIX WISCONSIN COUNTIES.[1]				
VALUE OF ESTATES IN THOUSANDS OF DOLLARS.	ESTATES OF GIVEN VALUE.			
	Number.	Percentage of Total Number.	Value in Thousands of Dollars.	Percentage of Total Value.
Under 0.5	1,570	67.323	589	5.304
" 1.0	1,644	70.497	642	5.781
" 2.5	1,809	77.573	928	8.356
" 5.0	1,970	84.477	1,561	14.056
" 7.5	2,078	89.108	2,168	19.522
" 10.0	2,153	92.324	2,785	25.078
" 15.0	2,219	95.154	3,573	32.174
" 25.0	2,269	97.298	4,418	39.783
" 50.0	2,302	98.713	5,534	49.834
" 100.0	2,314	99.228	6,369	57.353
" 500.0	2,330	99.914	9,861	88.798
All estates	2,332	100.000	11,105	100.000

The comparison is most easily made by reference to the Lorenz curves in Figs. 4 and 5. These graphs demonstrate clearly that, whether we consider the population as a whole, or only the richest three per cent of the men, the distribution bears a striking resemblance to that found to exist a decade earlier in Massachusetts. True, there is not quite as great inequality in Wisconsin as existed in the New England State but the difference is not at all startling, in fact, is less than one would anticipate in two different

[1] Derived from Table XI.
[2] See note to Table X.

regions with conditions of industry differing as widely as is the case in these two sections.

The Lorenz curves possess the highest degree of utility and simplicity for comparing the **general phases** of the **relative** distribution of wealth. The very attributes that make these graphs especially useful for this purpose make them of less value for purposes of a detailed analysis and absolutely worthless if it is desired to make comparisons on an absolute rather than on a relative basis. Table XIII has been constructed with a view to bringing into stronger relief some of the more important facts.

For purposes of this comparison, it has been deemed best to divide the entire number of decedents into four classes: **the poor,** comprising 65 per cent of the people; the **lower middle class,** composed of the next 15 per cent of the inhabitants; the **upper middle class,** made up of the next 18 per cent in order of wealth; and **the rich,** who form the last 2 per cent of the population. This classification should be kept in mind for it will be adhered to throughout the remainder of this chapter. The reader will observe that these classes differ materially in numbers contained. The poorest class consists of those possessing little or no property except furniture, clothing, and personal belongings. The lower middle class includes persons having a little property—perhaps a thousand dollars' worth on the average. This amount is sufficient to be of help in tiding them over in cases of emergency but is not sufficient to yield them any noticeable income. The upper middle class consists of the well-to-do, possessing property valued at from

TABLE XIII

HOLDINGS OF DIFFERENT FRACTIONS OF THE POPULATION CLASSIFIED ACCORDING TO WEALTH.[2]						
Class of Population.	State and Date.	Percentage of Total Estates Owned by Class.	Average Value of Estate in Dollars.	Price Index for Period.[1]	Index of Real Value of Estate.	Real Value of Estate Compared to Mass. 1859–1861 as base.
Poorest, 65% of Population.	Mass. 1859–1861	6.5	$ 360	141.0	255	100.0
	Mass. 1879–1881	5.0	377	147.5	256	100.3
	Mass. 1889–1891	4.5	399	112.9	353	138.4
	Wis. 1900	5.2	381	110.5	345	135.3
Lower middle class, 65 to 80%.	Mass. 1859–1861	4.2	1,009	141.0	716	100.0
	Mass. 1879–1881	1.9	622	147.5	422	58.9
	Mass. 1889–1891	3.9	1,499	112.9	1,328	185.5
	Wis. 1900	4.8	1,524	110.5	1,379	192.6
Upper middle class, 80 to 98%.	Mass. 1859–1861	32.4	6,485	141.0	4,600	100.0
	Mass. 1879–1881	26.5	7,224	147.5	4,897	106.5
	Mass. 1889–1891	32.8	10,509	112.9	9,308	202.3
	Wis. 1900	33.0	8,730	110.5	7,901	171.8
Richest, 2%.	Mass. 1859–1861	56.9	102,500	141.0	72,696	100.0
	Mass. 1879–1881	66.6	163,415	147.5	110,800	152.4
	Mass. 1889–1891	58.8	169,550	112.9	150,190	206.6
	Wis. 1900	57.0	135,715	110.5	122,830	169.0

[1] Index for middle year of period. Bureau of Labor index of wholesale prices; base 1890–1899.

[2] Derived from Tables IX, X, XI, and XII.

$2,000 to $40,000—persons usually deriving a considerable share of their income from investments but dependent upon their own exertions for the major part of the same. The rich, or those having wealth of more than $50,000, are in a position to live mainly on their incomes from property if they so desire. The percentage of men who, just preceding their death, fell in each of these classes is extremely significant. The first point to be noted is the fraction of the total wealth possessed by each of these great classes of the population. When we look at the bars in Fig. 6, we perceive that, while the shares of wealth belonging to each class differ somewhat with time and location, nevertheless, the shares have, on the whole, remained remarkably constant in Massachusetts and do not differ materially from those in Wisconsin. The following statements apply to all the instances studied. The poorest two-thirds of the people own but a petty five or six per cent of the wealth and the lower middle class possesses a still smaller share. Thus, the poorest four-fifths of the population, own scarcely ten per cent of the total wealth of the land.

The upper middle class makes a better showing having about one-third of all the wealth in its possession. It is to this class, probably, that ideal conditions of property ownership can best be ascribed. Here, the resources on hand add greatly to the feeling of security from poverty in time of misfortune. The

income from the accumulated wealth is sufficient to
obtain many comforts and luxuries, yet it is not

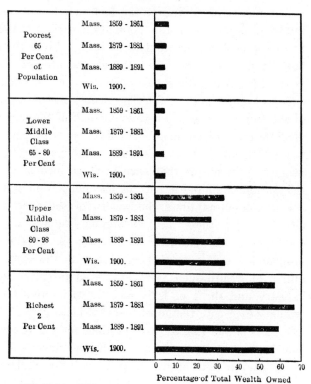

FIGURE 6

FRACTIONS OF TOTAL WEALTH BELONGING TO DIFFERENT
CLASSES OF THE POPULATION;[1]
MASSACHUSETTS 1859–1891, WISCONSIN 1900.

Percentage of Total Wealth Owned

[1] See Table XIII.

7

sufficient to tempt the recipient to a life of idleness or extravagance. The accumulations are not large enough to enable wealth to be used as an instrument of oppression or in the securing of great political power. It is this fraction of the population, then, for which the believer in democracy is likely to desire expansion.

The richest class, despite the fact that it includes but two per cent of the population, possesses the lion's share of the accumulated wealth. More than half, in fact, almost three-fifths of the property is possessed by this fiftieth part of the people. A reference to Fig. 5 shows us that the richest one per cent of the men dying owned almost one-half of the value of all the estates while one-fourth of the entire property was in the hands of one-four hundredth part of the people. This means that each of these men in the richest four hundredth part of the population possessed a hundred times the wealth of the average citizen. With these facts before us, we are in a condition to answer more intelligently the question propounded earlier in this chapter—"Is the distribution of wealth such as to act as an incentive to industry and thrift or is it such as to impress the ordinary man with the hopelessness of his situation?" The facts of the case seem to be that, for the young man having the average start in life, the chances are about one to four or five that he will accumulate property worth mentioning and about one in fifty that he will become moderately wealthy. It is, of course, true that, for the young man with scanty resources but with plenty of brains, the chances are far better than for the man under similar conditions but without much intelligence, but, in each case, the natural optimism of the average youth is likely to lead him to anticipate a far larger reward than his prospects actually justify him in expecting. Most of us are willing to take chances and trust to our lucky star and, since human nature is so constituted, it follows that property, as at present distributed, does act as a powerful incentive to effort and saving. Even the one chance in fifty of collecting a considerable fortune is, no doubt, a decided stimulus to a certain important fraction of the people but, with the majority, it is probably an insignificant factor as compared to the relatively so much larger chance of gathering together enough to buy the coveted home or secure the longed-for luxuries.

The differences between the classes are decidedly more striking than are the changes that have taken place. In the entire array, the only notable variation occurred in Massachusetts in the period 1879–1881 when the rich gained decidedly at the expense of the middle classes. In the next decade, however, the relative positions were once more resumed.

The most interesting comparison is that showing the absolute changes in the wealth of each of the four classes in Massachusetts and the relations, in each case, to the wealth of the same class in Wisconsin. For this purpose, it is necessary to take into consideration the change in the price level at the different dates. This correction having been made, we obtain the relative figures given in the last column of Table XIII. The graphic portrayal in Fig. 7 is more easily interpreted at a glance.

Fig. 7 shows that, during the thirty years, in Massachusetts, each class of the inhabitants became somewhat richer but, while the estates of the poorest increased by only about one third, those of the other classes were approximately doubled. The accuracy of this statement is open to some question, inasmuch as the wealth of the poorest part of the population was, in each case, principally estimated. It seems safe to say, however, that the rich have been growing decidedly richer but that the poor are not becoming poorer but are also gaining in wealth, though relatively at a less rapid pace than the rich.

No startling difference appears in the relative wealth of the different classes in Wisconsin as compared to Massachusetts, but it seems moderately certain that, in the older state, the rich are somewhat richer than in the newer commonwealth. The sharp decline in the wealth of the lower middle class, shown by the Massachusetts figures for 1880, is the one marked exception to the general trend of events.

FIGURE 7

THE RELATIVE WEALTH OF THE AVERAGE DECEDENT IN EACH
FRACTION OF THE POPULATION AS COMPARED WITH THE AVERAGE
WEALTH OF THE SAME FRACTION IN MASSACHUSETTS IN 1859–
1861.[1]

MASSACHUSETTS 1859–1861 = 100 PER CENT.

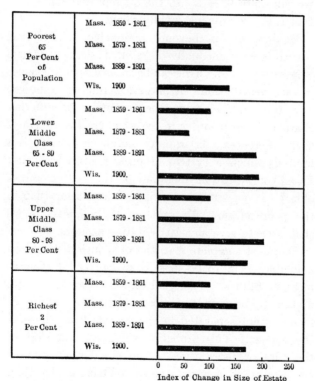

Index of Change in Size of Estate

[1] See Table XIII.

This illustration reiterates the fact brought out by the Lorenz graphs that, while wealth distribution is extremely unequal, there is no marked progress toward greater concentration in the hands of the few. We may believe that conditions are very bad, but we can scarcely establish the oft repeated contention that they are growing rapidly worse.

Having shown beyond reasonable doubt that wealth is very unequally distributed, the next logical step is to see if any light can be thrown upon the cause of such distribution. A natural method is to inquire into the conditions in other countries of differing characteristics in order to see what are the effects of such differences. Is property more concentrated in a land in which a system of primogeniture prevails? Does concentration increase as the nation grows older? Is it greater or less in the rich nation than in the poor nation? To some of these questions we shall seek to give at least tentative answers.

The most complete statistics of wealth distribution available seem to be those compiled by the government of France. There, all estates, large and small, appear to be listed. Unfortunately, the estates of men are not separated in the records from those of the women. This probably will affect but slightly the relative distribution but it will doubtless make the estates, in general, appear a little smaller than they really are as compared to the estates of Massa-

chusetts or Wisconsin, for the probated estates of
women probably average a little less in value than
those of the men. Presumably, however, rather a
small fraction of the women have estates worth
probating.

TABLE XIV

DISTRIBUTION, ACCORDING TO VALUE, OF ESTATES PROBATED IN FRANCE IN 1909.[1]				
Value of Estate in Francs.	Number of Estates in Class.	Value in Millions of Francs of All Estates in Class.	Percentage of Total Number of Estates.	Percentage of Total Value of Estates.
Excess of debts.............	13,897	—	3.533	—
1 to 500...	103,438	26.96	26.301	.470
501 " 2,000...	101,178	129.94	25.722	2.264
2,001 " 10,000...	110,427	543.25	28.076	9.464
10,001 " 50,000...	48,755	1,026.51	12.396	17.881
50,001 " 100,000...	7,692	529.56	1.956	9.224
100,001 " 250,000...	4,822	758.74	1.226	13.218
250,001 " 500,000...	1,720	605.66	.437	10.551
500,001 " 1,000,000...	810	554.40	.206	9.658
1,000,001 " 2,000,000...	373	512.17	.095	8.922
2,000,001 " 5,000,000...	145	425.61	.037	7.414
5,000,001 " 10,000,000...	46	303.30	.012	5.284
10,000,001 " 50,000,000...	10	179.94 } .003		3.135
50,000,001 and over.......	2	144.40		2.515
Totals.................	393,315	5,740.44	100.000	100.000

The levying of the inheritance tax results, in the
United Kingdom, just as in France, in the compilation
of statistics of estates. However, the figures for

[1] *Annuaire Statistique* for 1910, p. 221. This is practically a
complete record of all estates probated in France. The percentages have been computed by the present author.

estates under £100 are much less complete than those for the poorer classes of France. Two assumptions were made in the construction of Table XVI: first, that the estates of the poorest class of men averaged £60 each; and second, that the women owned the same fraction of the number and value of estates as in Massachusetts in 1890. The last assumption is probably faulty but it does not affect the relative distribution in any material way. Table XVII is derived directly from Table XVI.

The only available clue to the distribution of

TABLE XV

DISTRIBUTION, ACCORDING TO VALUE, OF ESTATES PROBATED IN FRANCE IN 1909.[1]				
Value of Estate in Francs.	Number of Estates.	Value of Estates in Millions of Francs.	Percentage of Total Number of Estates.	Percentage of Total Value of Estates.
Excess of debts..........	13,897	—	3.533	—
500 or less.........	117,335	26.96	29.834	.470
2,000 " "	218,513	156.90	55.556	2.734
10,000 " "	328,940	700.15	83.632	12.198
50,000 " "	377,695	1,726.66	96.028	30.079
100,000 " "	385,387	2,256.22	97.984	39.303
250,000 " "	390,209	3,014.96	99.210	52.521
500,000 " "	391,929	3,620.62	99.647	63.072
1,000,000 " "	392,739	4,175.02	99.853	72.730
2,000,000 " "	393,112	4,687.19	99.948	81.652
5,000,000 " "	393,257	5,112.80	99.985	89.066
10,000,000 " "	393,303	5,416.10	99.997	94.350
50,000,000 " "	393,313	5,596.04	99.997	97.485
All estates..............	393,315	5,740.44	100.000	100.000

[1] Computed from preceding table.

wealth in Prussia is obtained from the records of the property tax which are closely connected with those of the income tax.

TABLE XVI

THE ESTIMATED[1] DISTRIBUTION OF WEALTH AMONG MEN OVER TWENTY-FIVE YEARS OF AGE DYING IN THE UNITED KINGDOM, 1907–1911.

Value of Estate.	Number of Estates in Class.	Value in Millions of Pounds of all Estates in Class.	Percentage of Total Number of Estates.	Percentage of Total Value of Estates.
Less than £100............	162,311	9.74	79.23	4.57
£ 100 but under 500	22,320	7.72	10.89	3.62
500 " " 1,000	6,818	6.75	3.33	3.17
1,000 " " 10,000	10,920	47.56	5.34	22.31
10,000 " " 25,000	1,478	30.12	.72	14.13
25,000 " " 50,000	548	24.67	.27	11.57
50,000 " " 75,000	180	13.82	.09	6.48
75,000 " " 150,000	162	21.15	.08	9.92
150,000 " " 250,000	55	13.08		6.13
250,000 " " 500,000	32	14.45		6.78
500,000 " " 1,000,000	11	9.96	.05	4.67
1,000,000 and over........	5	14.19		6.65
Totals...................	204,840	213.21	100.00	100.00

Since estates under 6,000 marks in value are untaxed and unrecorded and since the great majority

[1] Sources of information—*Statistical Abstract of the United Kingdom for 1911*, p. 42, and the *Reports of the Registrar General on Births, Deaths, and Marriages in England, Wales, Scotland, and Ireland.* It has been assumed that women own the same share of estates in England as in Massachusetts. This assumption may be faulty but no figures are available. The figures have been averaged for the five years 1907–1911 inclusive.

of the families possess property less in value than
6,000 marks, all estimates are subject to a very large
margin of error.   It is believed that Tables XVIII and
XIX represent, however, a fairly good approximation
to the facts of the case, considering the meagerness

TABLE XVII

THE ESTIMATED DISTRIBUTION OF WEALTH AMONG MEN OVER TWENTY-FIVE YEARS OF AGE DYING IN THE UNITED KINGDOM, 1907–1911.[1]				
Value of Estate.	Number of Estates.	Value of Estates in Millions of Pounds.	Percentage of Total Number of Estates.	Percentage of Total Value of Estates.
Less than £ 100........	162,311	9.74	79.23	4.57
" " 500........	184,631	17.46	90.12	8.19
" " 1,000........	191,449	24.21	93.45	11.36
" " 10,000........	202,369	71.77	98.79	33.67
" " 25,000........	203,847	101.89	99.51	47.80
" " 50,000........	204,395	126.56	99.78	59.37
" " 75,000........	204,575	140.38	99.87	65.85
" " 150,000........	204,737	161.53	99.95	75.77
" " 250,000........	204,792	174.61	99.98	81.90
" " 500,000........	204,824	189.06	99.99	88.68
" " 1,000,000........	204,835	199.02	99.99	93.35
All estates................	204,840	213.21	100.00	100.00

of the data upon which one must rely.   The estimates
in Tables XV, XVII, and XIX are graphically compared in Figs. 8 and 9.

From these graphs, we discover the interesting
fact that there appears to be no marked difference
in the distribution of wealth in France or Prussia in

[1] Computed from preceding table.

1908 from that in Wisconsin in 1900. In other words, two old nations, one a monarchy and the other a republic, show approximately the same distribution as that occurring in a state in the Mississippi Valley and we have seen the close accord in this respect between Wisconsin and Massachusetts.

TABLE XVIII

THE DISTRIBUTION OF WEALTH AMONG PRUSSIAN FAMILIES, ESTIMATED FROM TAX ASSESSMENTS FOR 1908.[1]				
Family Wealth in Marks.	Number of Families in Class.	Wealth of Class in Billions of Marks.	Percentage of Total Number of Families.	Percentage of Total Amount of Wealth.
Less than 6,000	10,994,000[2]	15[3]	85.880	13.76
6,000 and under 20,000	871,000	9	6.804	8.26
20,000 " " 52,000	627,000	18	4.897	16.51
52,000 " " 100,000	169,000	12	1.320	11.01
100,000 " " 200,000	77,900	11	.608	10.09
200,000 " " 500,000	42,200	13	.330	11.93
500,000 " " 1,000,000	12,749	9	.100	8.26
1,000,000 " " 5,000,000	7,213	14	.056	12.84
5,000,000 " above	662	8	.005	7.34
Totals	12,801,724	109	100.000	100.00

[1] Computed from *Die Zeitschrift des Königlichen Preussischen Statistischen Landesamts*, pp. xxii, xxiii, xl.

[2] The remainder of the estimated heads of families and independent single persons in Prussia.

[3] Estimated from a curve, the assumption being that the curve for small properties would resemble in form that known to exist for France.

TABLE XIX

THE DISTRIBUTION OF WEALTH AMONG PRUSSIAN FAMILIES, ESTIMATED FROM TAX ASSESSMENTS FOR 1908.[1]				
Family Wealth in Marks.	Number of Families.	Wealth in Billions of Marks.	Percentage of Total Number of Families.	Percentage of Total Amount of Wealth.
Less than 6,000...	10,994,000	15	85.880	13.76
" " 20,000...	11,865,000	24	92.684	22.02
" " 52,000...	12,492,000	42	97.581	38.53
" " 100.000...	12,661,000	54	98.901	49.54
" " 200,000...	12,738,900	65	99.509	59.63
" " 500,000...	12,781,100	78	99.839	71.56
" " 1,000,000...	12,793,849	87	99.939	79.82
" " 5,000,000...	12,801,062	101	99.995	92.66
All families..........	12,801,724	109	100.000	100.00

A reasonable explanation of this striking similarity is the supposition that, given a competitive system of industry and trade and similar laws of property and contract, wealth tends to be distributed in proportion to certain natural qualities inherent in the human mind. If this supposition is true, it might naturally be expected that, at a certain stage of political organization, countries of similar racial characteristics would show similar shapes in the Lorenz curves illustrating the division of property.

Granting, however, that this hypothesis is correct, it by no means follows that there is a **natural** distribution of wealth. A modification of the laws of a

[1] Computed from Table XVIII.

FIGURE 8

A COMPARISON BY LORENZ CURVES OF THE ESTIMATED DISTRI-
BUTION OF WEALTH IN DIFFERENT COUNTRIES

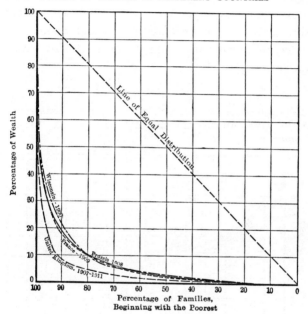

nation might bring into being a division of riches of
a radically different nature, for all property is a result
of law and, hence, its ownership may be modified
without limit if the ruling class so desires.

If we look at the Lorenz curve for England, as
shown in Figs. 8 and 9, we see this fact forcefully
called to our attention. The less equal distribution

is quite striking—the poor are relatively much poorer
and the rich are decidedly richer than in the other
countries. Both Great Britain and Massachusetts
are manufacturing nations; their people are racially
similar; in most respects their laws and customs are
much alike; why, then, this difference in the relative
dispersion of wealth?

FIGURE 9

A COMPARISON BY LORENZ CURVES OF THE DISTRIBUTION
OF WEALTH AMONG THE RICHEST FAMILIES IN VARIOUS
COUNTRIES.

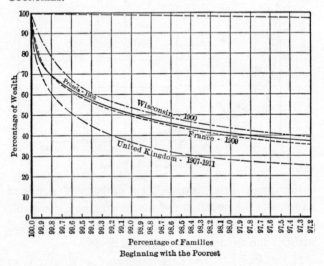

The answer is probably to be found in the laws of
inheritance. The English system of primogeniture

as regards landed property has kept the bulk of the estates intact in the hands of the oldest son with the natural result that there has been a tendency for these estates to increase continuously. In Prussia, France, and Wisconsin, all the children have shared more or less equally in the property of the parent; hence, estates have been broken up and there has been less concentration of wealth. If this presumption is correct, we have evidence of the powerful influence of inheritance laws upon wealth distribution and a means is suggested for such regulation as may be deemed desirable.

Having compared the general distribution of wealth in Wisconsin with that in European countries, the next step is to make an analysis similar to that used in comparing Wisconsin and Massachusetts. We shall again divide the total number of estates into the four classes, poor, lower middle, upper middle, and rich. The percentages for each nation will be identical with those previously used in the two American states, but, naturally, the average wealth of the persons in similar classes will differ according to the country of residence. Table XX brings out the principal points in the comparison. Fig. 10 shows graphically the difference in the shares of wealth possessed by identical fractions of the population in the various countries.

Again, we note the striking dissimilarity in the

percentages of total wealth retained respectively by
the vast majority and the small minority. In every
instance, the richest two per cent of the people own
considerably more property than all the rest of the
population. In England, the concentration is so

TABLE XX

THE MONEY VALUE OF PROPERTY OF DIFFERENT FRACTIONS OF THE POPULATION IN VARIOUS COUNTRIES.				
Class of Population.	Country and Date.	Percent-age of Total Wealth Owned by Class.	Average Value of Estate in Dollars.	Money Value of Estate Compared to Wisconsin, 1900, as a Base.
Poorest, 65% of the Population.	Prussia 1908......	4.9	153	40
	France 1909	4.3	186	49
	U. Kingdom 1909..	1.7	133	35
	Wisconsin 1900...	5.2	381	100
Lower middle class, 65% to 80%.	Prussia 1908......	5.5	743	49
	France 1909......	5.6	1,052	69
	U. Kingdom 1909 .	2.9	979	64
	Wisconsin 1900 ...	4.8	1,524	100
Upper middle class, 80%–98%.	Prussia 1908......	30.6	3,445	39
	France 1909......	29.4	4,602	53
	U. Kingdom 1909 .	23.7	6,670	76
	Wisconsin 1900 ..	33.0	8,730	100
Richest, 2%.	Prussia 1908......	59.0	59,779	44
	France 1909......	60.7	85,500	63
	U. Kingdom 1909 .	71.7	181,610	134
	Wisconsin 1900...	57.0	135,715	100
All classes.	Prussia 1908......	100.0	2,026	42
	France 1909......	100.0	2,817	59
	U. Kingdom 1909 .	100.0	5,067	106
	Wisconsin 1900 ...	100.0	4,762	100

great that this one-fiftieth part of the people own
nearly three times as much as the poor and middle
classes combined. In fact, the titles to half the
property of the United Kingdom are apparently in

FIGURE 10

FRACTIONS OF THE TOTAL WEALTH BELONGING TO DIFFERENT
CLASSES OF THE POPULATION IN VARIOUS COUNTRIES.

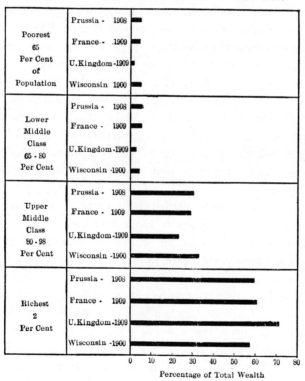

the hands of only half a per cent of the population. While this degree of concentration is worse than in the other countries, in Prussia and France, the richest one per cent of the owners held half of the wealth and, even in Wisconsin, we have seen that half the wealth belonged to only one-fiftieth part of the people.

In no instance, does the poorest sixty-five per cent of the inhabitants control much more than a twentieth part of the property and, in the United Kingdom, they possess but about a sixtieth part of the whole. Even the lower middle class owns but a trivial fraction of the wealth, varying from less than a thirtieth of the whole in the United Kingdom to about one-eighteenth in the French Republic. For all practical purposes, four-fifths of the population may be rightly pictured as being forced to satisfy themselves with the scraps of wealth cast aside from the table of Dives.

A more accurate picture of the property conditions of the various classes is given in Fig. 11. In this illustration, the relative wealth is represented by cubes whose volumes are, in each case, proportional to the money values of the holdings. In the United Kingdom, the little cube representing the average wealth of almost two-thirds of the people could be removed from the massive cube standing for the average wealth of the rich without causing much more than a nick in the corner and the same would

FIGURE 11

RELATIVE MONEY VALUE OF THE PROPERTY HELD BY THE
AVERAGE FAMILY IN EACH FRACTION OF THE POPULATION.

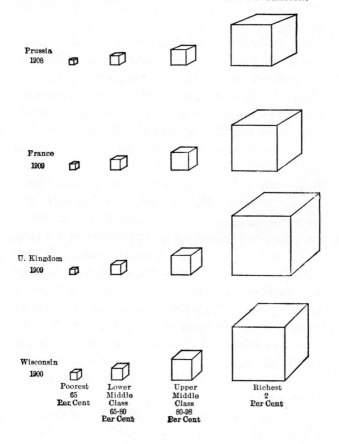

hold true to a slightly less degree in each of the other countries. In the great civilized nations, then, most of the wealth is in possession of one-fifth of the inhabitants but this does not mean that the benefits of property are circumscribed to the same extent. Even the lower middle class enjoys to a considerable degree the first advantage of wealth ownership—viz. the power to provide against emergency and disaster. They also receive to a certain extent, the second advantage of private property—freedom of movement—but this only accrues in full measure to the upper middle class. The lower middle class hold to their limited possessions with even greater tenacity than do the rich to theirs; for, as a man grows poorer, the utility of a dollar increases in far greater ratio than the diminution of his wealth. As a result, even the small property possessed by the lower middle class tends to render its members stable and law-abiding and strongly opposed to all forms of anarchy and violence. Hence, the first three advantages of private property from the social standpoint apply to most of the upper third of the population. For the lower two-thirds, all of these are absent. Only the fourth advantage of private property—the stimulus to wealth accumulation—affects the poorest two-thirds of the people.

Turning to the private standpoint, we see that only a small minority—the upper middle class and the rich—possess enough property to derive any considerable income therefrom to supplement the proceeds of their toil.

The question is still with us: "Is this a satisfactory condition of affairs?" There seems to be practically no doubt that it would be highly desirable for a far larger amount of wealth to be possessed by the poor. But wealth does not come by wishing and the supply is very clearly limited. Would it be better for the nation to take from the rich and give to the poor? Would this result in the poor proceeding to squander the accumulated capital of years in a brief revel of luxury and debauchery? Would the scattered wealth prove ineffective as a producing power and so reduce the national dividend as to decidedly increase the poverty of the very classes the dispersion was expected to benefit? [1] Or, on the other hand, could the wealth be taken from the rich and so utilized for the benefit of the poor as to raise their standard of

[1] Dr. Richard T. Ely's observations on his recent visit to New Zealand led him to believe that the abundant opportunities open to all in that prosperous region had tended to emphasize the distinction between the active and the passive elements of the population. The chance for rapid advancement had urged the virile on to more strenuous endeavors but the same opportunity for ready gains had made the easy-going man indolent and a poor workman. The author believes that the same phenomenon has been characteristic of the American frontier. This factor must, then, be taken into consideration in deciding whether a more equal distribution of property would or would not be conducive to greater production of wealth.

living, decrease the birth rate among them, increase
their saving power, and eventually build up a nobler
and better democracy?   At present, evidence appears
to be too scanty to render possible any definite answer
to these questions and the policy which one advocates
will depend on the way he, individually, decides upon
these propositions.

It should, however, be emphasized that wealth
distribution is the result of law and hence may be
modified in any way that the majority of the voters
deem best.   We have seen that, in Great Britain,
the law of primogeniture has apparently been responsible for greater concentration than exists in
other nations in which property is more equally
divided among the heirs.   If wealth can be concentrated by law, it might equally be dispersed by law.
For example, an inheritance tax might be used to
confiscate or greatly reduce large bequests and
inheritances and, if this were done, the tendency to
gather together wealth into great aggregations would
be decidedly less than at present.   It would also be
feasible to limit greatly, by law, the various opportunities for wealth to gain wealth.   Limitations might
be placed on investments in things that have proved
particularly profitable to the man of large means, for
example, public utilities, manufacturing plants, city
real estate, etc.   Speculative manipulation and the
typical methods of the promoters of high finance

might be prohibited or curtailed. In fact, in a hundred ways, legislation might be used to secure greater equality of possessions. If we deem the present gross inequality decidedly evil, then remedial legislation can be enacted none too soon.[1]

AVERAGE WEALTH

One more point should be noted before we leave the comparison of the wealth of different nations; that is the relative average wealth of the people in different countries. In this connection, all figures have been based on money values. No attempt has been made to compare the purchasing power of money in different nations but the investigations of the British Board of Trade do not show this to be at all radically different. In fact, with comparatively easy exchange of money and goods between nations, large differences can only exist in those commodities which are practically non-transportable or are guarded by high tariff duties. Since tariff duties are mutual, the net differences resulting therefrom are probably small. It seems likely, therefore, that the differences in the purchasing power of a dollar are not great enough to affect in any vital way the validity of the main conclusions derived. The wealth of each class in Wisconsin has been taken as 100. In the last

[1] For many of the preceding ideas as to the relationship between law and the distribution of wealth the author acknowledges his indebtedness to Dr. R. T. Ely's work on *Property and Contract*.

column of Table XX, the other nations are compared therewith. The results are shown graphically in Fig. 12.

FIGURE 12

A Comparison for Identical Fractions of the Population of Various Countries of the Average Money Value of Property per Family Relative to that of Families Comprising the Same Fraction of the Wisconsin Population in 1900.[1]

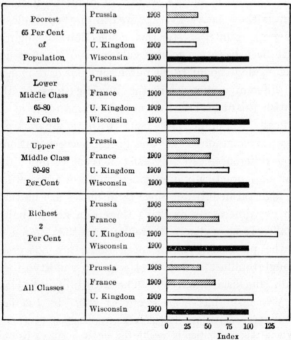

L. Money value of property of each class in Wisconsin =100

That wealth distribution is not at all closely connected with wealth per capita is brought out by the relation existing between conditions in France, Prussia, and Wisconsin. While, in all three countries, the relative shares of like fractions of the population are similar, there is a marked discrepancy between the average wealth per inhabitant in the different regions. The United Kingdom is the wealthiest nation of all, a fact which lends support to the theory that unequal distribution tends to saving and hence wealth accumulation. This idea is further reinforced by the knowledge that the average income of the inhabitant of the British Isles is undoubtedly materially less than that of the average person in Wisconsin.

Despite the fact, however, of the high average wealth, the masses of the people in the United Kingdom are poorer than the same classes in the other nations studied, possessing little more than a third as much property as the like fraction of the people of Wisconsin. In every class except the British rich, Wisconsin has a long lead in per capita wealth. This suggests the greater ease of wealth accumulation in a new country possessing abundant resources and we shall later see that the income obtainable in such regions is so much larger as to render it far easier to accumulate property. Of the nations studied, the statistics show that, on the whole, Prussia is the poorest nation with France not much better off.

CHAPTER V

INCOME DEFINED

In an earlier chapter, we discussed the various ideas concerning wealth. Now wealth and income are so closely related that great difficulty has been experienced by most writers on economics in keeping the ideas distinct. Income usually is held to consist of wealth and wealth is nearly always the result of income. In just what way, then, do the two concepts differ?

The one fundamental distinction is that income always represents a flow and not an accumulation and a flow can never be measured unless time is taken into consideration. Income, therefore, must invariably be measured as a given amount during a definite period of time.

The term income is applied to flows differing widely in nature and quality. A workman's wages, interest on loans, the rent of land, and the profits of a business man are all classified as income. A man is said to receive income through gifts or inheritance, through a rise in the value of property in his possession, through winnings from lotteries or gambling, or from the sale of products which he himself manufactures or produces from the soil. In recent years, most economists have added to the income list those pleasures which a person receives from the use of free goods. A man enjoys a beautiful sunset. Does he not receive income as truly as the man who enjoys the Oriental rug in his home? One is free and the other costs money but both alike appeal to the man's sense of beauty.

When the statistician undertakes to measure incomes, he quickly discovers that he cannot apply the same yardstick to each of the varieties above described. The commonest method of income measurement is to use money units as denominators. We say that a man earned or "made" two thousand dollars last year but we do not mean that he actually received this amount in **money.** As a matter of fact, under modern business conditions, but a small fraction of the amount would normally be obtained in coin or currency. Most transactions of moment are made through the use of bank credit exchanged by means of checks and drafts. A large share of the two thousand dollars may merely represent appreciation in the money value of land or other property held as an investment. When we speak of money income, therefore, we do not mean income in money but rather income measured in terms of money.

Of recent years, bondholders and other creditors have discovered that income measured in terms of money may be only a phantom of the imagination.

The man buying a two per cent United States bond in 1896 and allowing the interest to accumulate to the present time would find that the principal and all the interest compounded for the eighteen years would not buy back as many commodities or as good a piece of real estate as he exchanged for the bond nearly a score of years ago. Money has depreciated and the money value of commodities in general has increased more than the two per cent each year which the bond returns as interest. The interest, therefore, has been nominal and not real. This shows us, then, clearly, that money income is something far less tangible than the business man usually believes. Sometimes a dollar gained means one thing, sometimes another. The workingman realizes this fact when he discovers that, though his wages have risen, the prices of food and fuel and the rent of his house have risen even more rapidly.

Since, then, the term income is used to cover such diverse ideas, it is necessary to apply modifying adjectives to the word and separate the meanings into logical classes. The following three varieties are probably the most important kinds of income.

I. Book Income (commonly known as money income).

This equals the value in money of the net receipts or gain, as shown by an accounting system, accruing, during a given period of time, to an individual, a family, or a business concern, from personal services, investments, or business transactions.

This is purely a business concept. A man's book income is not immediately affected by the use to which he puts it. He may consume it, give it away, invest it, or destroy it and the amount of the income is unchanged. Book income is an accounting concept, yet a man may have a book income who does not know how to keep accounts. An agricultural laborer's book income might appear something like this, if correctly stated.

```
Wages, $30 per mo. for 9 mos....................$270
Board, room, and washing furnished by employer..... 180
Profit on horse-trade.............................  10
Increase in value of town lot.....................  30
                                                  ———
    Total receipts................................$490
Interest on mortgage on lot.......................  20
                                                  ———
Net book income.....  ...........................$470
```

Observe that his board during the winter, which he pays for at the restaurant in the village, is not included in his book income. This is purchased with money already accounted for.

The measurement of income received for personal services is more simple than the ascertainment of the income from investments. A man's savings may be hoarded away or they may be invested in bank credit, securities, lands, factories, office buildings, a home, a motor car, furniture, clothing, food, or drink. In the first case, it is evident that no money income accrues except in those instances in which the hoarded articles increase in money value. Hoarded standard money could never yield a money income. It is equally clear that investments in securities, lands, and factories normally yield a money income. How is such an income computed? The following example is typical.

Value of building at close of year..............	$3,000	
Rent received during year.....................	300	
Total..................................		$3,300
Value of building at beginning of year..........	$3,070	
Repairs, insurance, taxes, etc.................	50	
Total..................................		$3,120
Net money income for year...................		$ 180

The above example applies to a business building; why is it not equally applicable to the residence occupied by its owner? Evidently, if the man has saved $3,000, he has the option of buying a residence or investing in a business building and using the income derived therefrom to pay rent on a residence. In both cases, the net results are about the same— the $3,000 furnishes a habitation in which its owner may live and, the use of the house being worth money, this must be regarded as a form of money income.

But, if this reasoning applies to a house, is there any reason why it will not apply with equal force to the use of a motor car, or even to the use of the coat which a man wears? Logically, there seems to be little distinction. If, by the same method of computation used for the building, a surplus appears, then, that surplus is just as truly a part of the money income of the owner as was the net balance in the example cited. However, in most minor articles of consumption, the life of usefulness is so limited that the value of the services rendered is but little greater than the depreciation during the period used as a unit, the result being that the net money income becomes a negligible factor. We do not, therefore, ordinarily include the interest on the cost of the clothing and groceries on hand as part of the money income of the private family. On the other hand, we find that most men consider an investment in a house and lot a very different matter from an expenditure for a suit of clothes or a phonograph. In the purchase of the home, its selling possibilities are usually an important consideration. Men think of the likelihood of disposing of it later at an advance, of the rent saved, of car-fare added or eliminated. The money spent for a residence is regarded, therefore, as an investment of a semi-business nature; while the purchaser of a book-case or a carpet for home use rarely seriously considers the selling value of these articles. Besides, a large fraction of the population do not own but rent their homes while but few rent their furniture and personal belongings. There is, therefore, much to be said in favor of including in money income the net value of the services rendered by very durable consumption goods like houses and, at the same time, excluding from consideration less durable articles such as furniture, food, and clothing. This is the course required by law in the assessment of incomes for taxation in the state of Wisconsin.

The preceding discussion has served to point out the fact that the concept of book or money income is far less simple than it appears at first thought. It has also been shown that while book income is always measured in terms of money, the purchasing power of money varies, hence, a thousand dollars of book income may render vastly different service at one given period than the same number of dollars at a different period. For example, prices have risen greatly in the last decade, and the man with a fixed salary of one hundred dollars a month finds his purchasing power steadily being curtailed. This fact has given rise to a demand for some measure of income which will, as far as possible, eliminate results of value fluctuations in the medium of exchange. To accomplish this end, index numbers have been constructed which are intended to measure the price changes in commodities; actual book incomes have been divided by these index numbers; and the results have been used to compare the net loss or gain in purchasing power experienced by the individual income. This attempt to substitute the value of **many commodities** for that of **money** leads to the consideration of the concept of commodity income, or income in purchasing power, which may be defined thus.

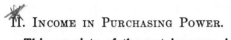

II. INCOME IN PURCHASING POWER.

This consists of the net increase in the power to obtain commodities or property, which accrues to an individual, a family, or a business concern during a given period of time.

In many instances, this practically amounts to a conversion of the book income into commodities. There is, however, one important exception to this rule. It arises from the fact that book income includes the increase in value of assets held during a period of time. Thus, if a man buys a piece of land for $1,000 and sells it two years later for $1,500, he would consider that he had gained a profit of $500. If, however, an inflation of the currency had caused other prices to double in the interval, he had really sustained a net loss in his ability to purchase commodities. The land had risen in value in respect to money but had fallen in value as compared to other goods. Such **fictitious** gains in assets may not, therefore, be legitimately included under the head of **income in purchasing power.**

9

Book income arising from wages, interest, or rent received, or from profits gained in mercantile or manufacturing operations, or from any other sources than increases in the market prices of assets, may be legitimately converted into terms of purchasing power through division by the correct price index. If a family's book income is $900 this year as compared to $800 last year, but if $900 will, this year, buy only as many commodities as could have been purchased last year with $750, then the income in purchasing power has evidently decreased and, from the economic standpoint, the welfare of the family has diminished. The amount of the purchasing power income is, therefore, of more importance to the recipient than the nominal figures shown on the books. This fact is generally recognized and hence the appellation **real** income has often been erroneously applied to this concept. However, real income is something materially different in nature as the following definition will help to make clear.

III. REAL INCOME (or psychic income).

Real or psychic income is made up of the amount of gratifications yielded by consumption of goods to an individual during a given period of time.

One observes that real income can accrue to an individual only, never to a group or organization except in an indirect way. The same amount of book income gives practically equal purchasing power to all persons in a given location at a given time but two men may sit side by side, at a concert, each paying two dollars for his seat; one may derive a great amount of pleasure from the performance, the other may go away bored. A motor ride may be a great treat to the poor child but extremely tiresome to the professional chauffeur. A dollar, in general, gives far less service to the very rich than to the very poor. We see, therefore, that book income and purchasing power income are, primarily, objective ideas while real income is, primarily, subjective in its nature.

It has been held by some writers that this definition of real income is too abstract and indefinite to be within the comprehension of most people. As a matter of fact, however, the ideas of book income and commodity income are decidedly more abstract than is this concept. The owner of a city home learns from the tax assessor's report and from current gossip that the selling value or the rental value of his property is increasing and, therefore, he is asked to pay more taxes. True, the house seems to be getting older and more in need of repairs, the trees are becoming scraggly and the lawn looks no better than in former years, yet, in some way, he is supposed to be attaining income through the rise in value. If he wishes to sell and move elsewhere, he finds that other houses have similarly increased in price and he cannot improve his condition by moving. His income received from the rising land value is, therefore, not only abstract but highly unreal.

Or let us suppose the case of a friendless man who by great care and self denial has succeeded in laying by five thousand dollars for his old age but dies before he has spent a dollar of the fund. To class this five thousand dollars as part of the income gained during his lifetime is of very doubtful validity. Aside from interest received, which appears in his annual income account, the only benefit which he has derived has been the added feeling of security experienced by having the money in the bank but he expected not only this satisfaction but also that he would derive much enjoyment from the goods purchased with the money. This part of his anticipated income never materialized and it, to most normal men, would be the most important part. The major part of the real income is likely to accrue to the heir for he benefits from the money. It seems, therefore, far more logical to speak of income as the effect upon the individual consciousness and to locate the time of income at the date when gratifications are received. Real income, therefore, is derived only in slight degree during the saving process but in full measure when the savings are expended.

The obvious conclusion seems to be that psychic income is a much more real and definite thing than either book income or commodity income. Were it, therefore, readily commensurable, it would be by far the most desirable basis for comparison. Unfortunately, it is not easy to measure. Units of pleasure received or pain averted are recorded in no way available for use by the statistician. Much real income arises from the use of free or public goods. How much of this account should be debited to individual A or to individual B? We cannot even obtain from our particular friends a fairly accurate estimate of their real income from free goods. Evidently, we cannot hope to record and tabulate such data for the nation as a whole. Practically, therefore, we must, in a statistical inquiry, consider only income in the form of economic goods and the preliminary measurement of such income cannot be made in units of gratification received but must be computed in money value. This method is, admittedly, far from ideal but it is the best available.

Fortunately, the error involved is not likely to nullify the worth of the inquiry. The fraction of income received by most people from free goods is, after all, a minor share and does not rapidly vary. Although a dollar is of more importance to the poor than to the rich man, yet, in a qualitative way, the incomes of the two are fairly comparable when measured in money. The man with a salary of four thousand dollars a year ordinarily receives less than

twice the real income of the man with a salary of
two thousand dollars, for the first two thousand
dollars is used to satisfy the more urgent wants, but,
nevertheless, he receives a larger real income. Furthermore, in the case of the most important comparison, that in respect to time, we are aided by the
fact, shown in the last chapter, that wealth distribution in the United States has remained fairly
constant for several decades. Human nature changes
but slowly. As a result, to the **average individual,**
at the same or different dates, two hats are likely to
give more satisfaction than one of like quality, two
pounds of candy ordinarily yield more pleasure than
one pound, and society is made up of individuals,
the majority of whom do not vary greatly from the
average. A record, therefore, of the quantities of
commodities actually consumed furnishes a reasonably good relative gauge by which to measure the
real income derived from economic goods. We are
primarily interested in comparing incomes at different
dates rather than in determining the absolute income
at a given time and, for the above reasons, the
income in purchasing power furnishes a fairly good
criterion of changes in real income.

Since incomes are necessarily computed on a money
basis, we shall first, in every case, attempt to apply
this standard. The next step is to reduce these book
incomes, whenever possible, to a basis of purchasing

power. In most instances, this can pe done with a
reasonable degree of success. It would be desirable
to complete the process by transforming the purchasing power income in each instance into real
income but, since this is impracticable, we must content ourselves with ascertaining book incomes or
incomes in purchasing power. As noted above,
changes of considerable amount in the last named
will probably be reasonably good indicators of the
change in the economic well being of the income
receivers.

Having thus briefly examined into the nature of
the income problem, we are now ready to proceed
with an inquiry concerning the incomes of various
classes of the people of the United States.

We have now considered the characteristics of income as dealt with from the standpoint of the individual recipients. These individuals compose society
and society is divided by geographical lines into
districts, counties, states, provinces, nations, etc.
This book deals, primarily, with only one nation,
the United States of America, and the aim is to estimate and analyze the total income which is received
by the people of this country as a whole. The
difficulties of measuring total real income are insur-
mountable, hence, the study will be confined to an
attempt to approximate the aggregate amount of
economic goods consumed, constituting what is

commonly referred to as the **national dividend,** and
to estimate the total quantity of goods produced by
the efforts of the people, an aggregate which we
shall designate as the **national income,** and to classify
this total according to the industries and factors of
production participating in its creation. The national
dividend, to speak with accuracy, consists wholly of
valuable services of persons or things. Our national
well being is measured by the amount of free or valuable services at our command. Most of us receive, to
some extent, direct services of other human beings.
Waiters bring us our food; our shoes are polished by
boot blacks; we are entertained by actors; our physical ailments are treated by physicians; lawyers aid
us with legal advice; and we are instructed by teachers
and clergymen. But the majority of people receive
only a minor part of their income in the form of
personal services. A larger fraction is made up of the
services of commodities. Our homes serve to shelter
us from the severity of heat, cold, and storm; our
clothing serves us by tempering the unpleasant effects
of sun and frost and wind as well as by catering to
our vanity. Our food tickles our palates and re-
plenishes our energies. All the gratifications, then,
which compose our real incomes are afforded by the
direct services of either persons or things. If the
services of free goods are omitted and all other
services are added together, they constitute the

national dividend. But, quantities of services, like quantities of gratifications, are difficult to measure and record. When we desire a small article, we usually buy the article itself rather than its separate services. On the other hand, when dealing with commodities of greater cost, we often invest in their services only. We do not purchase a street car line in order to enjoy the service of a street car—we purchase the service as we desire it; we often rent a house in which to live and even a piano by which to be entertained. In these cases, we receive the temporary services only, the title to the commodity, and hence its remaining services, resting in some other person. When a thing is bought outright, we capitalize, or roughly compute, the present worth to us of all the services which we expect the commodity to yield in the future. A dish of ice-cream renders brief service and disappears. The value of the service which it gives during the ten minutes in which it is being consumed is practically identical with the value of the ice-cream itself. This is an example of a very perishable article and perishable goods soon fail to give further benefit to the owner. On the other hand, one might be willing to pay only a dollar for the use of a piano for one evening and yet buy it outright at a price of three hundred dollars, for the buyer expects it to render services for years and, hence, the values of these individual services are discounted back to the present time and combined; the sum, which is the value to the purchaser, being at least equal to the price which he pays for the instrument.

When, therefore, a good is bought for purposes of consumption, the real thing purchased is a bundle of anticipated services. If the calculation is correct, the price paid for the article is likely to be approximately the present worth of all the future services. Since most consumable commodities are not very lasting, the larger share being used up within a year or two, if we know the value of the consumable commodities reaching the consumers of a nation during a year, we have an approximation to the value of the services received or, in other words, to the value of the national dividend. It is, then, possible, through changes in the supply of commodities and personal services to measure changes in the national dividend.

The total value of the **national dividend** differs materially from the **national income,** the latter being considered as the sum total of the book incomes of the inhabitants of a nation. The difference is of about the same nature as that existing between the net gain of a corporation and the dividends paid. The profits of the corporation for the year might be one million dollars but the directors might deem it advisable to lay aside half of the amount for expanding the business and only pay out half a million dollars in dividends. In the United States, every income receiver is, to a limited extent, a director when it comes to disposing of the national income. Each person may decide to lay aside a fraction of his income or he may spend the entire amount for current needs. Those who save increase, directly or indirectly, the capital supply or productive equipment of the nation. The part of the national income included in their savings does not, in any sense, form a part of the national dividend for the current year any more than does the amount invested by a corporation for improvements constitute dividends for the stockholders. Savings or investments are intended to enlarge the dividends of future years. The yearly savings of the people of the United States constitute a very considerable sum as is evidenced by the rapid growth in the capital supply of the country. If this large sum of total savings were subtracted from the total book or money income of the people, the remainder should be approximately equal to the value of the national dividend.

CHAPTER VI

THE NATIONAL INCOME AND THE INDUSTRIES
THAT PRODUCE IT

THE NATIONAL INCOME

FROM our farms and forests, out of our mines and rivers and lakes, from our shops and factories, and from our theatres, our schools, and our churches flows forth a constant stream of finished commodities and services ready for consumption by the people. It is the result of natural forces and materials being utilized or acted upon by man's efforts. It includes the final products of the capitalistic processes of industry. From this stream, if at all, the wants of all the people must be satisfied. It is to the enlarging of this stream that the energies of the nation are primarily directed.

In addition to this stream, whose annual flow constitutes the national dividend, there is produced, each year, a quantity of new capital goods, much greater than that used up by the industrial processes. This additional capital represents the savings of the nation. These savings, together with the national dividend, constitute the national income—the total product of the efforts of the citizens.

We shall consider first this great national income stream as a whole, and later the changes that have taken place therein during the last sixty years.

With existing data, it is difficult, if not impossible, to estimate with great accuracy the total value of the national income at any given date. Two methods of attack are available: first, a study of the consumption of the people; second, an investigation into the production of the nation. Owing to the nature of the existing data, the second method is probably more workable in practice. This is due to the fact that we have little reliable information concerning the prices of goods sold at retail.

Fairly accurate records of wholesale prices are easily obtainable but we have no means of readily ascertaining the percentages added to these prices by various middlemen before the commodities reach the hands of the final consumer. This percentage is probably variable to a considerable degree, hence the ratio of wholesale to retail prices might be quite different in 1910 from what it was in 1850. Besides, in the measurement of goods consumed, it is almost inevitable that more or less duplication will result, owing to the inclusion of the finished products of one industry among the raw materials of another. Thus, some cloth goes directly to the ultimate consumer but a large share is further manufactured by garment factories and tailors. Much flour is used by the housewife in her cooking but almost equally important is the percentage utilized by bakers. In the strictest sense, of course, the manufacturing process is not complete until the housewife has made the dress or baked the bread but, since we have no statistical record of the values added by the American housewives, it makes it impracticable to include their services in the computed value of the national dividend.

An attempt was made by the present writer to estimate the total value of goods consumed by the American people but the difficulties of obtaining reasonably accurate results were so great that the undertaking was abandoned in favor of another mode of attack. It might be said, however, that the crude estimates of consumption checked closely enough with those made by the method hereafter described to indicate that a sufficient expenditure of effort might result in arriving at a close approximation to the money value of the goods used up in each year by the people of the nation as a whole.

Two methods of approximating the total national income have suggested themselves: first, to multiply the average book income of the families in each class of the population by the number of families composing the respective class, then adding together the products; second, to trace the process of production from nature to the final consumer. The first plan was tried for 1910 and the totals did not differ greatly from those obtained by the other method. The second mode of procedure proved, however, to require less guessing and to conform far more closely to the limits of existing reliable data. It, therefore, has been adopted as the principal *modus operandi* for this chapter. It becomes necessary, then, to explain this plan in some detail.

Natural resources often possess value just as they exist in mine or forest or soil. In the first process of rendering these resources available for human needs, there is constantly being added the value of labor and capital used up in extracting them together with certain profits for the entrepreneur. The raw materials thus produced go in large part to the factories. Here, their value is again increased by labor, capital, and entrepreneurs. Meantime, our transportation agencies, principally wagons, vessels, and railways, must be recompensed for moving things from place to place. Later, the merchant adds value to the goods by holding them in readiness to serve the convenience of his customers. Incidentally, industry is kept properly in operation through the aid of physicians, teachers, lawyers, clergymen, and government officials. Their pay must be added to the expenses of production. There is also an army of men and women employed in producing services by comparatively direct methods. This army includes waiters, barbers, tailors, baseball players, actors, musicians, and others who give personal service that immediately satisfies our wants. All of their efforts must be rewarded. In the end, the combined products of these varied activities unite to form the national income. The capitalist lays aside the part that is saved while the ultimate consumer must pay for the much larger share used in the direct satisfaction of wants. The aggregate bill of the final consumer is identical with the value of the national dividend. We must, in this connection, be careful to avoid the apparently common impression that the ultimate consumers form one class of the population and the producers another. Most of the adult population of the country fall under both heads, while small children and the few persons of parasitic leisure constitute the small group who may correctly be classed as consumers only.

The final estimates of the total net book income of the people of the United States appear in the second column of Table XXI. Since savings are included, the amounts are materially larger than the aggregates of the national dividend for the various periods. This table, as illustrated by Fig. 13, shows the remarkable record of an increase of the national income, by the year 1910, to about fourteen times its value in 1850 with the per capita share more than trebled. In the present period of rising prices, some one will

TABLE XXI

						Dollars' Worth of Purchasing Power at Average Prices of 1890 to 1899.[4]	
Census Year.	Total Money Income in Millions of Dollars.[1]	Per Capita Income in Dollars.	Average Size of Family.[2]	Family Income in Dollars.	Index of Price Level.[3]	Per Capita.	Per Family.
1850	2,214	95	5.6	535	139.2	69	384
1860	3,636	116	5.3	613	141.3	82	434
1870	6,720	174	5.1	889	221.6	79	401
1880	7,391	147	5.0	735	132.4	111	555
1890	12,082[5]	192	4.9	941	113.6	169	828
1900	17,965	236	4.7	1,109	101.7	232	1,090
1910	30,530	332	4.5	1,494	126 5	262	1,181

THE ESTIMATED INCOME OF THE PEOPLE OF THE CONTINENTAL UNITED STATES.

[1] The figures in this column are summaries of the estimates for the various industries as shown in Table XXIII. The mode of estimation was as follows: To the value of the products of the extractive industries (agriculture, fishing, and mining) was added the value imparted to these products by the processes of manufacture, transportation, holding for sale, etc. The services of the government were assumed to be worth the amount paid for running the government. The estimated value of the direct services of persons and of residence property was added. To avoid duplication, building costs were deducted since the income from buildings later appears as either business or residence "rentals." The remainder constitutes the national income.

The information is almost entirely derived from the United States Census. The results are believed to be moderately accurate. The errors for 1900 and 1910 should not be greater than ten per cent. The earlier census figures are believed to be much less accurate and the error probably increases gradually as the time distance from the present increases. Even the figures for 1850, however, are probably within twenty-five per cent of the correct results.

10

be sure to suggest that this is only an **apparent**
increase due to the change in the price level.   This is
in no sense true, as is shown by the last two columns

FIGURE 13

ESTIMATED AVERAGE PER CAPITA INCOME MEASURED IN MONEY
AND PURCHASING POWER FOR THE CONTINENTAL
UNITED STATES

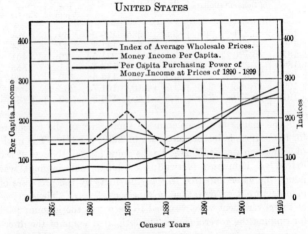

Census Years

[2] *Abstract of the United States Census for 1910*, p. 259.

[3] Wholesale price index reduced to base 1890–1899 from the
Aldrich Report on Wholesale Prices, Part I, p. 91, and from *Bulletin
114 of the United States Bureau of Labor Statistics*, p. 149.   Price
level given for year preceding date of census.

[4] Money income divided by the price index and multiplied
by 100.   The cost, at average prices of 1890–1899, of the goods
which could be purchased with the money income received in
the given year.

[5] Estimated by Charles B. Spahr in *The Present Distribution of
Wealth in the United States*, p. 105, at $10,800,000,000—about
11% less.

in which price changes have been eliminated by dividing the income by the index of wholesale prices. The adjustment merely accentuates the change, showing that the period has seen the purchasing power of the income of the average individual more nearly quadrupled than trebled. The only reverse movement occurred in the ten years from 1860 to 1870 and this was probably due to the destructive effects of the Civil War, though it is possible that the apparent decrease during this decade resulted from the 1870 Census returns from the South being inadequate, owing to the disturbed condition of that section of the country.

But a large share of the income of the people has not been consumed from year to year but has been laid aside to increase the capital funds of the country. This is evidenced by the rapidly increasing wealth of the United States as set forth in Chapter II. True, part of this wealth increase has been nominal and represents only increasing land scarcity but a larger proportion consists of a real increase in capital. It is worthy of note, however, that rising land values constitute a growing fraction of the nominal increase in the wealth of the people of the nation for, in the decade 1850–1860, only a little over a third, while, in the last decade, nearly three-fifths of the recorded increase in riches consisted of higher land values.

The National Dividend

By deducting the total capital savings from the book income, we arrive at the national dividend. Table XXII gives us a very rough estimate of the total savings and of the value of the goods actually consumed by the people.

TABLE XXII

The National Dividend for the Continental United States Measured in Purchasing ower. Estimates Based on Production.						
Census Year.	Estimated Total Income in Millions of Dollars.[1]	Estimated Capital Savings in Millions of Dollars.[2]	Net Goods Consumed in Millions of Dollars[3]	Index of Price Level.	Value at Prices of 1890–1899 of all Goods Consumed.	
					Total in Millions of Dollars.	Per Capita in Dollars.
1850	2,214	400	1,814	139.2	1,303	56
1860	3,636	843	2,793	141.3	1,977	63
1870	6,720	1,047	5,673	221.6	2,560	66
1880	7,391	1,267	6,124	132.4	4,626	92
1890	12,082	1,612	10,470	113.6	9,218	146
1900	17,964	1,569	16,395	101 7	16,121	212
1910	30,529	2,000	28,529	126.5	22,552	245

It must not be supposed that all increases in land values are due to growing land scarcity. Much of the higher value of land is due to improvements

[1] See Table XXI.

[2] Estimated by deducting from the average annual increase in wealth for the decade, the average annual increase in land values for the same period.

[3] Column 2 minus column 3.

therein such as clearing, drainage, better transportation facilities, etc. Only part of these improvements are accounted for under the head of railway and government expenditures, etc.

The fact was brought out in a preceding chapter that the wholesale price index is not adequate to reduce accurately money incomes to a basis of purchasing power. Nevertheless, any possible error involved is far too slight to offset the striking growth here shown.

There are two other forces, however, which undoubtedly tend to lessen the importance of this great increase in money income. The first of these is the disappearance, in a large measure, of the services of free goods—services which formerly played a much more important part in the life of the American people. The second is the transfer of the process of production from the home to the factory. The most of the value added by the housewife has always escaped the census taker but, in the times when the majority of the articles consumed by the family had obtained a large part of their utility through her efforts, this omission was of far greater importance than in these days when so many of our housewives patronize the steam laundry and buy clothing ready made and food ready cooked and when sewing and bread making are tending, like spinning and weaving, to join the ranks of the lost arts. Women still toil but, more and more, their work has been transferred from the kitchen to the office or factory. In this way, they have entered the ranks of the "gainfully employed" and the products of their labor appear regularly in the Census tables.

But, after all reasonable allowances have been made, the fact remains, practically, that, beginning with 1870, there has been an increase in the national dividend so enormous that it cannot logically be ascribed to anything but the tremendous advance in productive power due to the revolutionary improvements in industry which have characterized the last half century. It seems improbable that any other great nation has ever experienced such sweeping gains in the average income of the inhabitants. It has, almost necessarily, been accompanied by a great rise in the standard of living. The increase has not been so much in the quantity as in the quality of the goods thought of as necessaries by the average citizen. Today, the urban housewife, for example, looks upon running water, a bath room, electric lights, a gas range, and a piano as necessary household equipments. She demands that her food be purchased not in bulk, but in air-tight sanitary packages. She does not care to go to market but expects her purchases to be delivered in small amounts at frequent intervals. She must have clothing not only sufficient for comfort and neatness but also strictly à la mode.

Her children must not thumb dog-eared books and dirty slates while seated in a dingy little room on rough wooden benches in the presence of a pedagogue who pieces out his wages as a farm laborer by teaching "the three R's" during the winter. On the contrary, they must have an endless chain of interesting reading books, must write in pretty clean tablets, and must work with up-to-the-minute laboratory equipment under the direction of highly trained teachers in a beautiful, light, airy school room. Neither are the children expected to quit school when they have learned to "figger" and to parse. They must go to high school and become versed in the scientific knowledge of the day, with a little home economics, music, and manual training on the side. When supper is over, the children and their parents do not entertain each other or visit the neighbors, but instead hire the services of paid entertainers at the theatre or moving picture show or take a ride in the boat or car or automobile. No matter which way one turns, the demand is for better and better quality, more and more elaborate service, greater and greater variety.

And most of this is as it should be. If our great inventions and discoveries do not provide more luxuries for the average man, it is hard to see that they have been of any service to civilization. But, if they have resulted in uplifting the general standards of comfort, this service should be frankly recognized and we should appreciate the economic advantages which the new era of industry has enabled us to enjoy.

Of late, we have had a period of "muck-raking" in which all things that exist have been pictured as very bad and growing worse. The misery of life, the difficulty of making both ends meet, has been over-emphasized. True, it is just as difficult to secure the articles required by our standard of living as it ever was. But, our standard of living has grown more expensive. Increases in quality cost even more than increases in quantity. Our wants always have and probably always will increase with our ability to satisfy them so that there is never any hope of winning the race with our standard of comfort. Such a race is just like chasing one's shadow. Nevertheless, to the present author, a larger per capita supply of economic goods appears to be a most distinct benefit to any nation and the United States has been greatly favored in this line during the last sixty years.

Industrial Shares of the National Income

We have thus far considered the national income as a unit. Our next task will be to divide it according to its origin and study some of the separate segments. There are many parts to the great national mill that grinds out the finished products for our use. These parts may work smoothly as one huge, intricate machine or each industry may form together an independent unit almost disconnected with the other industries, and meeting them only as a trader in the markets of the world. The opposite extremes are illustrated by the goals of two branches of present day socialists. The national socialists would have all industry united under the control of the central government. The industrial socialists would have each industry a separate unit owned by the workers therein. Let us for the moment think of the great fields of industry from this latter point of view, separating out agriculture from manufacturing, manufacturing from mining, etc. Let us group together within each single industry its capitalists, proprietors, superintendents, foremen, and workmen and ascertain, if possible, the share of the total income stream which all of these persons, aided by their equipment, actually produce. How much does society gain from the efforts of the farmers and their families and employees? How large a value do the manufacturing interests add to the total net product? These queries are partially answered by Table XXIII and Fig. 14.

In order to compare more readily one industry with another, these figures have been reduced to percentages of the entire national income. The results appear in Table XXIV.

TABLE XXIII

The Estimated Industrial Distribution of the National Value Product, Shares Measured in Millions of Dollars Worth.[8]

Census Year.	Total Product in Millions of Dollars.	Government.[1]	Commercial and Professional Services.[2]	Manufacturing, Light and Power.[3]	Transportation.[4]	Fishing.[5]	Mining.[6]	Agriculture.[7]
1850	2,213.8	100.3	469.5	434.2	411.9	10.0	23.0	764.9
1860	3,635.6	161.7	791.2	801.0	718.6	12.9	62.0	1,088.2
1870	6,720.1	436.6	1,989.9	1,607.5	742.9	15.0	145.0	1,783.2
1880	7,390.7	458.3	2,473.7	1,803.5	927.4	33.8	218.0	1,476.0
1890	12,081.6	784.9	3,652.3	3,822.3	1,194.9	38.2	329.0	2,260.0
1900	17,964.5	1,469.0	5,466.9	5,125.3	1,581.8	42.5	591.0	3,688.0
1910	30,529.5	2,591.8	8,977.2	8,437.6	2,656.0	48.9	976.0	6,842.0

[1] Includes national, state, and local governments.

[2] Roughly estimated on the basis of a constant ratio to the product of urban population and average income.

[3] Value added by manufacturing process, less expense for fuel, building material, and other products of other industries necessary for upkeep of the plants.

[4] Gross earnings, less depreciation charges, fuel used, material used up for equipment, etc.

[5] Value of fish caught, less upkeep of vessels, nets, etc.

[6] Value of products sold, less new machinery and buildings and depreciation on capital goods employed.

[7] Value of products consumed on farms for direct satisfaction of human wants or sold to outside consumers; also includes rental value of residences less expenditures for building materials; deducts machinery and fertilizers purchased.

[8] For the distribution of the product of *each industry* to wages, interest, rent, and profits see Tables XXXa to XXXd in the Appendix.

FIGURE 14

ESTIMATED SHARES OF THE TOTAL VALUE OF THE NATIONAL
INCOME PRODUCED IN EACH OF THE PRINCIPAL FIELDS OF
INDUSTRY

in the Continental United States

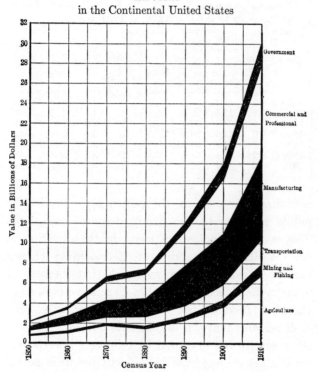

This table, and Fig. 15 which accompanies it,
bring out the fact that some industries have grown
decidedly at the expense of others. The government
is gradually absorbing a larger and larger share of the

TABLE XXIV

THE ESTIMATED[1] PERCENTAGES OF THE TOTAL VALUE OF THE NATIONAL INCOME PRODUCED BY EACH GENERAL FIELD OF INDUSTRY IN THE CONTINENTAL UNITED STATES.								

Census Year.	Government.	Commercial and Professional Services.	Manufacturing and Light and Power.	Transportation.	Fishing.	Mining.	Agriculture.	Total.
1850	4.5	21.2	19.6	18.6	.5	1.0	34.6	100.0
1860	4.4	21.8	22.0	19.8	.4	1.7	29 9	100.0
1870	6.5	29.6	23.9	11.1	.2	2.2	26.5	100.0
1880	6.2	33.5	24.4	12.5	.5	2.9	20.0	100.0
1890	6.5	30.2	31.6	9.9	.3	2.7	18.7	99.9
1900	8.2	30.4	28.5	8.8	.2	3.3	20.5	99.9
1910	8.5	29.4	27.6	8.7	.2	3.2	22.4	100.0

activities of the nation, the percentage expended for public purposes having nearly doubled since 1850. This seems to indicate a trend in the direction of state socialism. Despite the development of our immense transportation systems, that branch of industry has failed to maintain its relative rank as to value of product but has declined greatly. We shall see later that this decline does not show a falling off in service but is caused by relatively lower rates; while other commodities have fluctuated, transportation has steadily grown cheaper. Agriculture and fishing have also been unable to keep up with the procession though agriculture has been gaining for the

[1] Computed from Table XXIII.

last two decades. This is doubtless due to the price of agricultural products rising more rapidly than the prices of other commodities. Mining still furnishes a comparatively small part of the national income

FIGURE 15

ESTIMATED RELATIVE SHARES OF THE PRINCIPAL FIELDS OF INDUSTRY IN THE NATIONAL INCOME FOR THE CONTINENTAL UNITED STATES; MEASURED IN TERMS OF MONEY VALUE

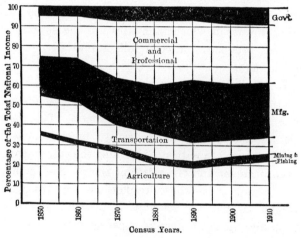

but it has been advancing more rapidly than any other great branch of industry. Manufacturing and general commercial and professional pursuits made rapid gains up to 1890 since which date they have declined somewhat. Their recent relative decline seems to be due to the rising value of products depending more directly on the land. Whichever way we turn, we discover growing land scarcity appearing as an important factor in distribution.

Having compared the different branches of industry with each other, the next step is to analyze each separately. Two leading questions come to mind: First, how do the value-products turned out by each worker compare in the different branches of industry? Second, by which of the different fields are the new wants of the consumers being mainly satisfied? In other words, in which industries are the supplies of articles produced for each inhabitant most rapidly increasing in quantity?

We shall first take up the consideration of a productive activity not usually considered as industrial, that is, the work of the government. The rising cost of this institution has caused much comment, largely adverse in nature, concerning the extravagance of government and the waste of the peoples' money. The rejoinder of those responsible for the taxes usually is that the country is growing and that, naturally, the governmental expenses must grow with it. If, by country growth, we mean increase in population, taxes have risen out of all proportion thereto. Table XXV reduces all expenses to a per capita basis and then eliminates changes due to the price level.

The last column shows us that, if taxes were settled for in commodities, it would require nearly seven times as much to pay the tax bill of the average individual as was required in 1850. Even though average income has nearly quadrupled, it has been far outstripped by government expeditures. The justification for increasing expenses of government

TABLE XXV

THE ESTIMATED CHANGES IN THE PER CAPITA EXPENSE OF GOVERNMENT FOR THE CONTINENTAL UNITED STATES.				
Census Year.	Expenses of Government in Millions of Dollars.[1]	Expense per Capita for Entire Population.	Price Level.[2]	Index of "Real" Expense per Capita.[3]
1850	100.3	$ 4.32	139.2	3.11
1860	161.7	5.14	141.3	3.64
1870	436.6	11.32	221.6	5.11
1880	458.3	9.14	132.4	6.90
1890	784.9	12.47	113.6	10.99
1900	1,469.0	19.33	101.7	19.01
1910	2,591.8	28.18	126.5	22.28

can not, then, lie in the growth of the country but must be made, if at all, on the ground that government today is taking over the functions formerly left to private industry and is giving vastly greater service to the citizen of today than the citizen of sixty years ago received from the government of his day.

[1] See Table XXIII.

Wholesale prices for year preceding the census.

[3] Expense in dollars if commodities had remained at the prices of 1890 to 1899.

TABLE XXVI

THE ESTIMATED CHANGES IN THE TOTAL PRODUCTION AND IN THE PER CAPITA PRODUCTION AND SUPPLY OF MANU-FACTURED ARTICLES IN THE CONTINENTAL UNITED STATES.

Census Year.	Total Value Produced in Millions of Dollars.[7]	Index of Prices of Manu-factured Arti-cles.[1]	Index of Quantity of Manu-factured Articles.[2]	Index of Quantity per Capita for Total Popula-tion.[3]	Thousands of Persons Employed in Manu-facturing.[4]	Index of Quantity Produced per Person Engaged in Manu-facturing.[5]
1850	434.2	137.8	315.1	13.59	957	329
1860	801.0	129.7	617.6	19.64	1,311	471
1870	1,607.5	191.7	838.6	21.75	2,054	408
1880	1,803.5	122.9	1,466.9	29.29	2,733	537
1890	3,882.3	112.7	3,445.0	54.73	4,552	757
1900	5,125.3	100.7	5,090.0	66.98	5,716[6]	891
1910	8,437.6	123.9	6,810.1	74.05	8,025[6]	849

Table XXVI shows the tremendous growth which has taken place in the production of manufactured articles. The value has been divided by the price index for manufactured goods in order to eliminate

[1] Base 1890–1899; *Bulletin 114, United States Bureau of Labor Statistics*, p. 14, and estimated from *Senate Report 1394*, Part 1, on *Wholesale Prices*, p. 91.

[2] Millions of dollars' worth at prices of 1890–1899.

[3] Dollars' worth at prices of 1890–1899.

[4] *Statistical Abstract of the United States for 1912*, p. 776.

[5] Dollars' worth at prices of 1890–1899.

[6] Estimated from the *Abstract of the United States Census for 1910*, pp. 438–9.

[7] Value added by manufacturing processes less expenditures for advertising, insurance, etc., which have been included under "Commerce."

fluctuations in the price level. By the fourth column of the table, we see that over five times as large a supply of manufactured articles is now turned out for each person in the United States as was produced in 1850. The workers in industry have become more efficient, each one, on the average, producing more than two and a half times as much as in 1850. We shall later see that wages have risen in a somewhat similar ratio, though this would by no means necessarily follow, for the capital supply per laborer has been greatly increased during the period.

The figures given on page 439 of the *Abstract of the United States Census for 1910* indicate the following investment per wage earner for the different census years.

1850............	$ 557	1890............	$1,535
1860............	770	1900............	1,850
1870............	825	1910............	2,706
1880............	1,021		

Unless, then, the modern productivity theory is sadly in error, we should naturally anticipate the increase in product per laborer, shown in the last column of Table XXVI, but we should also be surprised if labor continued to receive as large a share of the product as formerly.

Table XXVII gives a similar view of the changes in the productivity of transportation by rail, water, and wire. Unfortunately, we have no good statistics

11

of the prices of transportation before 1890. Since that date, freight and passenger charges are accurately computed for the steam railways but not for street

TABLE XXVII.

THE ESTIMATED CHANGES IN THE TOTAL PRODUCTION AND IN THE PER CAPITA PRODUCTION AND SUPPLY OF WATER, RAIL, AND WIRE TRANSPORTATION FOR THE CONTINENTAL UNITED STATES.							
Census Year.[8]	Total Value Produced in Millions of Dollars.[1]	Average Railway Freight Rates per Ton Mile in Cents.[2]	Estimated Index of Rates for All Transportation.[7]	Index of Total Quantity of Transportation.[4]	Quantity of Transportation per Capita for Entire Population.[5]	Persons Employed in Transportation in Thousands.[6]	Index of Quantity Produced per Person Engaged in Transportation.
1850	411.9	3.74	3.10	120.3	5.19	—	—
1860	718.6	2.93	2.49	261.3	8.31	—	—
1870	742.9	3.02	2.48	271.3	7.04	348	780
1880	927.4	1.47	1.38	608.6	12.13	496	1,227
1890	1,194.9	.934	1.00	1,082.0	17.19	809	1,337
1900	1,581.8	.724[3]	.811	1,766.2	23.24	1,079	1,637
1910	2,656.0	.763[3]	.830	2,898.0	31.51	1,744	1,661

[1] See Table XXIII.

[2] For years 1850 to 1890 a simple average of average rates for different railways—*Senate Report 1394*, Part 1, pp. 615–617.

[3] *Statistical Abstract of the United States for 1912*, p. 324.

[4] Approximate value in millions of dollars at prices of 1890–1899.

[5] Approximate value in dollars at prices of 1890–1899.

[6] Estimated from statistics of railway employees in the *Statistical Abstracts of the United States* and from the *Census of Occupations for 1900*, pp. xxxvi–lvii.

[7] Passenger rates have not been lowered as rapidly as freight rates.

[8] Figures for year preceding census.

FIGURE 16

ESTIMATED OUTPUT IN DIFFERENT FIELDS OF INDUSTRY PER
PERSON EMPLOYED

Measured in Dollars Worth at Prices of 1890–1899 for the Continental United States

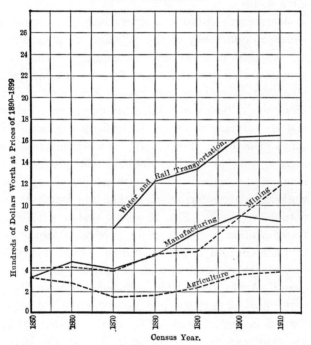

railways and vessels. The index given in column four is, therefore, very unreliable before 1890, and since that date, is representative only of the major product, railway carriage. The railway business,

however, is such a dominant factor in transportation
and the changes have been so great that there seems
to be no doubt of the steady and rapid fall in shipping
rates during the last half of the nineteenth century.
This stands in sharp contrast to the fluctuating prices
in other commodities and shows mainly the greater
increase in efficiency of the railways and steamships
as compared to other lines of industry. While the
manufacturing industries are turning out for each
inhabitant five times the product that they did in
1850, the railways and ships are doing even better
and are carrying six times the traffic per person that
they did in 1850. Since 1870, railway workers have
succeeded in more than doubling the product per
man, an achievement closely paralleled by the
workers in manufacturing. While the **increases** in
output are similar, Fig. 16 shows that a worker in
transportation is much more productive than his
comrade engaged in manufacturing. Does this indicate a higher degree of skill or is there some other
cause? Again, the teachings of economic theory lead
us to suspect that the real cause for the difference
lies not in the inherent ability of the laborer but in
his more expensive equipment; that is, the larger
product represents the more important rôle played
by capital, rather than greater human efficiency.
On page 27, the *United States Census Report of 1904
on Wealth, Debt, and Taxation* estimates the total

value, in 1899, of railway property, street railways, canals, and ships at $11,248,500,000 or approximately $10,425 per employee, or more than five times the investment per employee in manufacturing. It is, therefore, not at all surprising that, with so much more expensive equipment, the product per man is about double what it is in manufacturing.

TABLE XXVIII

THE ESTIMATED CHANGES IN THE TOTAL PRODUCTION AND IN THE PER CAPITA PRODUCTION AND SUPPLY OF MINERAL PRODUCTS FOR THE CONTINENTAL UNITED STATES.

Census Year.	Total Value Produced in Millions of Dollars.[1]	Index of Prices of Mineral Products.[2]	Index of Quantity of Mineral Products.[3]	Quantity of Mineral Products Per Capita for Entire Population.[4]	Persons Employed in Mining in Thousands.[5]	Index of Quantity Produced per Person Engaged in Mining.[6]
1850	23	164.8	14.0	.60	34	412
1860	62	144.2	43.0	1.37	101	426
1870	145	232.2	62.4	1.62	163	383
1880	218	135.9	160.4	3.20	296	542
1890	329	109.2	301.3	4.79	529	570
1900	591	109.8	538.2	7.08	603	892
1910	976	127.0	768.5	8.36	645	1,191

[1] See Table XXIII.

[2] Simple average indices of prices of "Metals and implements" and "Fuel and lighting," *Bulletin 114, United States Bureau of the Statistics of Labor,* p. 149; *Senate Report 1394,* Part 1, p. 99. For year preceding the Census year.

[3] Millions of dollars' worth at prices of 1890–1899.

[4] Dollars' worth at prices of 1890–1899.

[5] *Census of Mines and Quarries for 1902,* p. 6.

[6] Dollars' worth at prices of 1890–1899.

The productiveness of the mines is set forth in Table XXVIII. The increase in the gross product has been much more rapid than in any other great field of industry having been multiplied by fifty in the course of six decades. The product per worker has likewise increased, at a rate somewhat similar to that shown by manufacturing and transportation.

TABLE XXIX

The Estimated Changes in the Total Production and in the Per Capita Production and Supply of Agricultural Products for the Continental United States.						
Census Year.	Total Value Produced in Millions of Dollars.[1]	Index of Prices of Agricultural Products.[2]	Index of Quantity of Agricultural Products.[3]	Quantity of Agricultural Products Per Capita for Entire Population.[4]	Persons Employed in Agriculture in Thousands.[5]	Index of Quantity Produced per Person Engaged in Agriculture.[6]
1850	764.9	97.5	784.5	33.82	2,404[7]	326
1860	1,088.2	119.8	908.4	28.89	3,331[7]	273
1870	1,783.2	204.7	871.2	22.59	5,949	146
1880	1,476.0	114.9	1,284.5	25.61	7,714	167
1890	2,260.0	111.5	2,027.0	32.21	8,566	237
1900	3,688.0	100.0	3,688.0	48.54	10,382	355
1910	6,842.0	153.1	4,469.0	48.60	11,389	392

[1] See Table XXIII.

[2] For year preceding census. See *Bulletin 114 of the United States Bureau of Labor Statistics*, p. 149, and *Senate Report 1394*, Part 1, p. 107.

[3] Value in millions of dollars at prices of 1890–1899.

[4] Dollars' worth per capita at prices of 1890–1899.

[5] *United States Census of Occupations*, pp. l–liii.

[6] Dollars' worth at prices of 1890–1899.

[7] Slaves not included.

It will be observed from Fig. 16 that the last decade has witnessed a decided increase in the quantity of product per worker in the mines, while, in the other fields of activity, there has been only a slight change during the same period. The reasons for this are not clear but the probable cause is the decided improvements in mining methods brought about by the more general introduction of power machinery. According to the statements of the United States Census, the reports on capital invested in mines have too wide a margin of error to prove of great value.

FIGURE 17

ESTIMATED RETURNS PER CAPITA FROM DIFFERENT FIELDS OF INDUSTRY

Measured in Dollars Worth at Prices of 1890–1899 for the Entire Population of the Continental United States

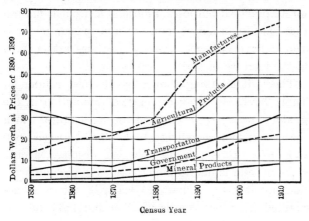

Census Year

While the products for each person in the country have, in other industries, been increasing at least five times in amount, Table XXIX shows that the per capita supply of agricultural produce has less than doubled in sixty years. This accords with the well-known economic law that, as income increases, the demand for food increases much more slowly. Our wants for subsistence are comparatively soon satisfied. Under these circumstances, any large excess of agricultural produce would have little utility at home and so, naturally, would be exported— but we have failed to find the raising of agricultural products for export as profitable as other lines of industry and, hence, we have ceased to send food-stuffs abroad to any great extent. The demand for the products of mines and factories and railways is, for all practical purposes, limitless, hence it is natural that the expansion of industry due to new methods should have occurred along those lines rather than in the increase of agricultural produce.

The striking thing shown by the last column of Table XXIX is the very marked diminution in the product per person engaged in agriculture which the census figures indicate took place between 1850 and 1870. It is possible that the decrease is only apparent and is due to imperfections in the enumeration but it may, in part, at least, be otherwise accounted for. The census of 1850 and 1860 did not include slaves as persons enumerated; therefore, the per capita product in the South would represent the output of a freeman assisted by whatever slaves he owned. This would help to swell the average product per worker. Furthermore, the industry of the South was disorganized by the Civil War; the negroes probably did not prove efficient independent farmers; and, hence, we would expect the product per man to decrease decidedly before 1870. While these reasons in part explain the falling off in 1870 and 1880 it seems quite possible that the figures computed for those two years are somewhat too low.

CHAPTER VII

THE DISTRIBUTION OF THE NATIONAL INCOME
AMONG THE FACTORS OF PRODUCTION

IN the last chapter, we studied the way in which the great river of national income is produced by the various industries. Laborers, capitalists, landlords, and entrepreneurs, financiers, economists, and statesmen, all plan and contrive ways and means of increasing the flow. In this respect, their interests are one. When, however, it comes to the division of this bountiful stream into the branches and rivulets and rills that go to each class, industry, occupation, or individual, the unity of interest disappears and each group is likely to selfishly seek to increase its own share at the expense of the others.

It is evident that the economic welfare of the individuals composing each group or class will depend upon three things: first, the size of the stream; second, the share going to the group or class; third, the number of persons within the class among which the share is to be divided. Any study, then, of the relative progress of any segment of the population involves a consideration of these three points.

Economists have been wont to divide the products of industry into four parts, viz. rent, interest, wages,

154

and profits; these being the payments for the services of the four factors of production—land, capital, labor, and the entrepreneur, respectively. Some economists have disputed the advisability of this division but it still persists and is, in many respects, a useful classification. One of the aims of this chapter will be to ascertain what share of the income is actually received by each of these factors. Under the head of rent, we shall place all recompense for the use of natural resources but none of the hire of buildings or improvements. Wages is taken broadly to include all payments to employees for their services, whether they work for $500 or $50,000 per year. By interest, is understood the necessary amounts paid in order to obtain the use of capital goods, and capital goods are usually defined as those products of man's efforts used in the further production of wealth. Examples of capital goods are warehouses, office buildings, stores, machines, livestock, raw materials, and stocks of merchandise. Payments for the use of any of these or increases in their value due to holding them until the time when needed for use are classed as interest.

The term profits comprises the entire share which the entrepreneur receives for his personal efforts in carrying on the business in which he is engaged. It does not include interest on the capital or rent for the land which he has invested in the enterprise but does cover all payments for his own services whether physical or intellectual. The salary which he could command if employed by others is commonly known as the entrepreneur's wage. This, together with all chance, speculative, or monopoly gains is comprehended under the head of profits, as here defined. For instance, after a farm owner has charged off rent for all land used, wages for his hired hands and his children who help him, and interest for all capital goods employed, the balance of his net earnings consists of profits.

Information is far too limited to enable us to make the apportionment between these four shares with any great degree of accuracy. Fortunately, we have fairly good wage statistics covering the fields of manufacturing, mining, and railroading and, even in agriculture, statistics of moderate quality are available. We are, therefore, enabled to compute the share of labor with a fair degree of certainty that the errors are of slight consequence; and, after all, this is the share about which there is most inquiry at present.

The Share of Land.

Rent has been estimated as a percentage of the value of the land. This involves an error in that it fails to account for the fact that land value represents the total present worth of future as well as of present rentals, and so takes account of increases in the rent which are expected to occur later. In a new country, where steadily rising rents are normally anticipated, the value of land is considerably greater than that obtained by capitalizing the present rent at current interest rates. An attempt has been made to offset any error from this source by using the low rate of four per cent of the value as an estimate of the rent of the land

In computing the share of interest, the rates have been taken as from six to eight per cent of the estimated value of existing capital goods. Since there is no uniformity in the Census reports concerning the things classed as capital, the estimate of the total value of capital goods is necessarily a very crude one.

The remainder of the total product has been entered under the head of profits. The author realizes that some economists would prefer to class monopoly gains with rent but it was not feasible to do so in this case, even if such a course were desirable.

To sum up, it is believed that the share of wages is rather accurately set apart, that the share of rent is close enough to the reality to answer some of the questions commonly asked about it, and that the division of the remainder of the total net product between interest and profits, though admittedly very inaccurate, yet is as close to the facts as can easily be estimated from the Census material and indicates the truth in a broad way. The general estimates appear in Table XXX and the salient features are brought out by Fig. 18.

TABLE XXX

THE ESTIMATED TOTAL NATIONAL INCOME FOR THE CONTINENTAL UNITED STATES DIVIDED INTO RENT, INTEREST, PROFITS, AND RETURNS TO EMPLOYEES.						
CENSUS YEAR.	AMOUNT IN MILLIONS OF DOLLARS.[2]					PRICE INDEX.[1]
	Total.	Wages and Salaries.[3]	Interest.	Rent.	Profits.	
1850	2,213.8	792.8	276 5	170.6	973.9	139.2
1860	3,635.6	1,351 1	532.6	321.2	1,430.7	141.3
1870	6,720 1	3,269.5	864.5	463.2	2,122.9	221.6
1880	7,390.7	3,803.6	1,373.2	642.3	1,571 6	132.4
1890	12,081 6	6,461.8	1,738.9	913.8	2,967.1	113.6
1900	17,964.5	8,490.7	2,695.7	1,396.0	5,382.1	101.7
1910	30,529 5	14,303.6	5,143.9	2,673.9	8,408.1	126.5

CENSUS YEAR	PURCHASING POWER, BASE, 1890-1899.					
	Total.	Wages and Salaries.	Interest.	Rent.	Profits.	
1850	1,590.5	569.6	198.6	122.6	699.7	
1860	2,572.8	956.2	376.9	227.3	1,012.4	
1870	3,032.4	1,475.3	390.1	209.0	958.0	
1880	5,582.3	2,873.0	1,037.2	485.1	1,187.0	
1890	10,635.5	5,688.2	1,530.9	804.4	2,612.0	
1900	17,665.9	8,349.6	2,650.9	1,372.9	5,292.5	
1910	24,137.0	11,309.9	4,066.4	2,113 8	6,646.9	

[1] Wholesale prices for year preceding the census. *Bulletin 114 of the United States Bureau of Labor Statistics*, p. 149.

[2] The figures for wages and salaries are believed to be fairly accurate; those for rent are thought to have an error of not more than twenty per cent. The separation of the share of capital from that of the entrepreneur is very crudely done and no stress should be laid on the results. The total for all shares is thought to be more accurate than the mode of distribution and, for the

FIGURE 18

ESTIMATED DISTRIBUTION OF THE NATIONAL INCOME FOR THE
CONTINENTAL UNITED STATES AMONG THE FACTORS
OF PRODUCTION

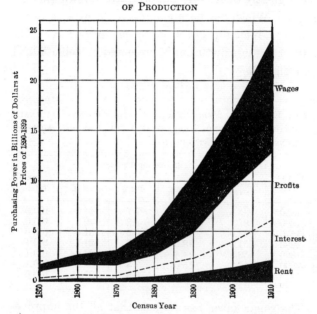

last three census years, should come within ten per cent of the
correct statement of the national income. For earlier years,
the error should not be over twenty per cent at the outside.

[3] Wages and salaries were independently estimated, also, by
the method of multiplying the estimated number employed by the
average wage received. The variations for the different years
between the respective results of the different methods are as
follows:—1850—4 per cent; 1860—5 per cent; 1870—5 per cent;
1880—7 per cent; 1890—1 per cent; 1900—2 per cent, showing
the improving accuracy of recent figures.

But, after all, absolute figures are of but little interest to most of us. Fig. 18 shows that all the shares have greatly increased; but we have known that already. Which has been gaining at the expense of the others? Which has been losing out in the race? The answer to these questions is presented in Table XXXI and Fig. 19.

TABLE XXXI

THE ESTIMATED PERCENTAGES OF THE TOTAL NATIONAL INCOME RECEIVED RESPECTIVELY BY LABOR, CAPITAL, LAND, AND THE ENTREPRENEUR.					
CENSUS YEAR.	SHARES OF PRODUCT.[1]				
	Wages and Salaries.	Interest.	Rent.	Profits.	Total.
1850	35.8	12.5	7.7	44.0	100.0
1860	37.2	14.7	8.8	39.3	100.0
1870	48.6	12.9	6.9	31.6	100.0
1880	51.5	18.6	8.7	21.3	100.1
1890	53.5	14.4	7.6	24.6	100.1
1900	47.3	15.0	7.8	30.0	100.1
1910	46.9	16.8	8.8	27.5	100.0

The single taxer has told us that all the improvements of industry result only in the enrichment of the landlord. A glance at Table XXX shows us how absurd this statement is. The value of our products has increased since 1850 to the extent of some twenty eight billions of dollars while rent has gained less than three billions. Evidently, it has captured but a very meager part of the new production. In fact, it

[1] Computed from Table XXX.

FIGURE 19

ESTIMATED RELATIVE SHARES OF THE DIFFERENT FACTORS OF
PRODUCTION IN THE NATIONAL INCOME FOR THE
CONTINENTAL UNITED STATES

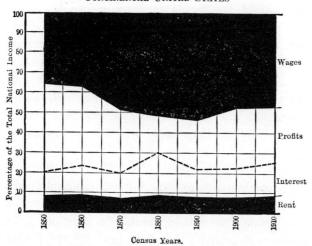

Census Years.

has only tended to keep its constant share of the
output, the percentage being the same in 1860 as
in 1910. As a matter of fact, the indications are
that rent plays a much less important rôle in distribution than the followers of Henry George would
have us believe. It is interesting, in this connection,
to note the relative size of the rent item and the
expenses of government. Reference to Tables XXV
and XXX shows us that, before the Civil War, the
rent bill was large enough to pay all governmental
charges nearly twice over. In 1910, however, the
12

rent would have been barely sufficient to pay off the various governmental budgets as at present constituted and, with the growing concentration of activities in the hands of government, it appears that rent will soon be a quantity far too small to meet the required charges. With increasing pressure on our natural resources, however, it is probable that the percentage of the total income paid for rent will gradually increase and, since this is true, the lag behind the growing governmental expenses will be considerably less than would otherwise be the case.

THE SHARES OF CAPITAL AND THE ENTREPRENEUR

The combined share of interest and profits showed a striking decline between 1860 and 1870 and has since tended to remain practically constant. The decline was probably largely a result of the freeing of the slaves and the destruction of capital due to the Civil War. When the slaves were largely transformed into wage earners, the natural outcome was a large increase in the wages bill at the expense of interest and profits. The industry of the South was so disorganized by the conflict that it took a number of years for business to get on its feet again; hence, the share of profits and interest was cut down even further though this effect was partially offset by the higher interest rates prevailing for the capital which escaped destruction.

THE SHARE OF LABOR

Since rent has constituted a share relatively stationary and comparatively unimportant in amount, wages have been practically the complement of the combined factors of interest and profits. The great rise of the share of wages during the decade 1860 to 1870 has therefore just been accounted for in explaining the fall of interest and profits. It will be noted that the rise in the percentage received by wages continued slowly until 1890 and has since been gradually declining. Is there any logical explanation of this change?

Statistical studies of the fraction of the total income going to wages are so rare that few if any laws on this score have yet been inductively formulated. Economists are not even united upon any deductive theory for this case. Any reasons assigned, therefore, must be purely hypothetical. The most probable causes for the decline of the last two decades are perhaps the disappearance of free land, with the attendant increase in the pressure upon our natural resources, and the great influx from abroad of labor of a low degree of efficiency. Whether these are or are not the correct explanations of the changing trend, the fact remains that the total share going to labor has, of recent years, been falling off despite the efforts of labor unions and combinations. It still remains a mooted question whether any labor organization not monopolizing practically the whole wage earning class can, through combination, cause a larger share of the total national income to be paid as wages than would fall to the lot of labor under a regime of free competition.

It is the worker's share of the product which seems to appeal most to the imagination of present day writers. This is the period in which "down-trodden labor" is at least coming to have its importance recognized. But the question of primary importance is not how much does **labor as a whole** receive but how much, on the average, does **each laborer** get. Is the worker being treated justly? Does the unskilled toiler receive a fair living wage? If not, how can his condition be bettered?

And these queries are rightly considered of the first importance. The overwhelming majority of our population are dependent primarily upon wages for their income and, therefore, the economic welfare of the nation is largely synonymous with the wages of the working people measured in purchasing power; in other words, it depends upon the extent to which the money wages received are adequate to furnish the necessities and customary luxuries of life.

But nothing is more futile than the denunciation of the employers as a wicked and heartless class because they refuse to pay higher wages. The employer is the slave of existing competitive conditions.

In the established and better understood industries, he cannot long pay higher wages for the same grade of labor than do his competitors or he will soon be forced to the wall. But these competitive conditions may be changed. They are the results of law and custom and society can, by legal enactment, largely revolutionize them at its pleasure. Suppose, that, by radical legislative changes, the largest possible fraction of the national dividend was diverted to the share of wages. How would it affect the wage earners?

In 1910, the wages bill of the nation was approximately $14,303,600,000. It is possible that the government might tax away all rent and turn the proceeds to the benefit of labor. Interest cannot be decreased without resulting in a loss of saving; hence, the interest bill could scarcely be lessened without destructive effects to the capital supply of the country, thus ruining our industries. Nothing, therefore, could be gained from that source. Average profits, as will be seen by reference to Table XXXII, are only about half as large again as average wages. We could not get the services of entrepreneurs for nothing and it must be conceded that the farmers and planters and business men, as a rule, rank higher in efficiency than does the average employee; therefore, these entrepreneurs must necessarily be paid somewhat more than the average wage of the latter.

Suppose, that, as the maximum possible allowance, we took one fourth of all profits and diverted those also to the benefit of the employees. The total allowance for wages and salaries would now amount to about $19,079,500,000, or a gain of almost exactly one third over and above the present payments for labor.

But not nearly all of this one third addition would be a gain to the income of the employed classes, for very many employees own land and derive a considerable fraction of their income from its rent. The commonest example of this is the case of home-owners who enjoy the services of the land on which their residence stands. Many others receive rent and profits indirectly through the ownership of the stocks or bonds of corporations. A few obtain profits through business ventures of their own. For these employees, the transfer of rent and profits to the wages fund means taking money out of one pocket and transferring it to another, though the amount lost might be greater or less than that gained. Thus, it would seem improbable that, with our present national productive power, any feasible system of distribution could increase the average wage earner's income in purchasing power by more than one fourth and this is an extreme rather than a moderate estimate. While such a change might or might not be desirable, it would, at least, work no startling revolution in the condition of the employees of the United States. The grim fact remains that the quantity of goods turned out absolutely limits the income of labor and that no reform will bring universal prosperity which is not based fundamentally upon increasing the national income. After all, the Classical Economists were right in emphasizing the side of production in contradistinction to that of distribution. Nature refuses to yield her bounty except in return for effort expended. Demands for higher wages have never yet unlocked her storehouses.

We have talked about the possibilities, through a new system of distribution, of increasing the income of the laboring classes. We have observed that labor has been fairly successful in retaining about a half of the total product, but this tells us nothing about the portion going to each individual and the last is a question of vastly more importance than the study of the share obtained by labor *en masse*. Has the compensation for the efforts of the average laborer increased as fast as should be the case considering the tremendous improvements in industrial processes? Has the entrepreneur distanced the employee in the race, constantly securing the lion's share of the added spoils? Some light will be thrown upon these questions by reference to Table XXXII and Fig. 20.

The fact should be emphasized that the distinction

between employees and independent entrepreneurs is very far from being definitely ascertainable from the Census tables, and, as a result, the figures cited in Table XXXIIa of the Appendix must be taken as mere approximations. They only represent an attempt to apportion as accurately as possible the total number of persons in the United States reported by the Census as gainfully employed. Columns four

TABLE XXXII

Census Year.	Index of Price Level.[1]	Total Wages and Salaries in Millions of Dollars.[2]	Number of Employees in Thousands.[3]	Average Money Wage per Employee per Annum.	Average Wage per Employee in Purchasing Power.[4]	Total Profits in Millions of Dollars.	Number of Entrepreneurs in Thousands.	Average Money Profits in Dollars per Entrepreneur.	Average Profits per Entrepreneur in Purchasing Power.[5]
1850	139.2	792.8	3,880	$204	147	973.9	2,200	443	318
1860	141.3	1,351.1	5,090	265	188	1,430.7	3,150	454	321
1870	221.6	3,269.5	8,240	397	179	2,122.9	4,270	497	224
1880	132.4	3,803.6	11,790	323	244	1,571.6	5,600	281	212
1890	113.6	6,461.8	16,220	398	350	2,967.1	7,100	418	368
1900	101.7	8,490.7	20,350	417	410	5,382.1	8,720	617	607
1910	126.5	14,303.6	28,200	507	401	8,408.1	9,350	899	711

THE ESTIMATED RETURNS FOR PERSONAL EFFORTS IN THE CONTINENTAL UNITED STATES.

[1] United States Bureau of Labor wholesale price index for year preceding the Census.

[2] See Table XXX.

[3] See Table XXXIIa in the appendix.

[4] Purchasing power of the money wage at the prices of 1890–1899.

[5] Purchasing power of the money profits at the prices of 1890–1899.

FIGURE 20

ESTIMATED AVERAGE ANNUAL RETURN TO ENTREPRENEURS
AND EMPLOYEES[1]

Measured in both Money and Purchasing Power.
Base 1890–1899

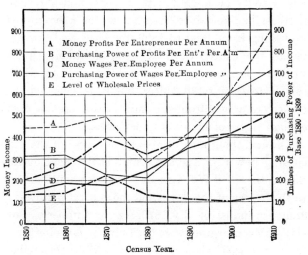

and eight in Table XXXII are taken from Table
XXXIIa. The fact has already been noted that
column seven, denoting total profits, is a rough
approximation only. The methods of estimation,
however, were such as to cause the errors to be somewhat similar in percentage and direction from year
to year and, as a result, the general tendencies shown
should not be very far from the truth.

[1] Calculated from the United States Census Reports for the
Continental United States.

Both money wages and money profits have been reduced to a basis of purchasing power by dividing by the price indices for the respective years. The result represents the dollars' worth of commodities which could be bought with current money receipts if prices had remained constant at the average level prevailing from 1890 to 1899, the base used throughout by the United States Bureau of Labor. Again, we have been compelled to use the index of wholesale instead of retail prices but it is believed that the errors arising from this substitution are not great enough to be of material importance.

The first thing noticed about the course of the purchasing power of average profits is the great decline during the Civil War period. This was doubtless due to the freeing of the slaves and the general paralysis of Southern industry. By 1870, a great number of poverty-stricken negroes were beginning to farm for themselves and their scant gains would still further reduce the average of profits. The slight decline shown for the next decade is probably due to the business depression prevailing in 1879, the year to which the census figures for 1880 really apply. From 1880 to 1900 average profits increased enormously, almost trebling in amount and far outstripping average wages in purchasing power. It must, however, be remembered that, in 1880, profits were far below normal for it is almost inconceivable that it would be possible to continuously secure the services of entrepreneurs at a lower rate than that paid for employees. For fifty years, the general trend of wages and profits has been upward, and at about the same rate, with profits per man normally standing at perhaps fifty or sixty per cent more than the average amount paid to employees. This does not indicate that entrepreneurs, in general, are grossly overpaid for their aid in the process of production. Some of the great captains of industry undoubtedly secure princely incomes as a reward for their personal efforts but they are far from typical. Most entrepreneurs are farmers, small merchants, or shop keepers, hotel proprietors, and the like, and, if the incomes from their investments in land and capital are subtracted from their net gains for the year, the few hundred dollars remaining for each man can scarcely be pictured as the reward of a plutocrat.

It will be noted that the fluctuations of wages in purchasing power, as shown by graph D in Fig. 20, are much less violent than the changes in profits. It is the entrepreneur who takes the risks of industry. He is the buffer who withstands the shocks of business depression and panic. The workingman's wage, therefore, receives a degree of protection by no means accorded to the recompense of his employer.

Throughout the half century, the earnings, measured in commodities, of the average employee showed a most gratifying increase, practically trebling in the five decades. Even the depression, caused by the great monetary expansion and the consequent high prices of the Civil War period, was almost overcome by 1869 and, from that date on, each decade marked a striking advance.

The Census figures represent total wages paid for the year. The picture which they give, then, is indicative of the general rise in the laborer's greatest source of income—his wages. As far as representing the prosperity of the worker is concerned, yearly earnings are better than a record of daily or monthly wages, for the annual wage takes full account of the fact that he may have been unemployed much or little during the year while daily or hourly wage statistics tell us nothing whatever in this respect. The well being of the laboring class is, therefore, far more dependent upon the total wage for the year than upon the hourly pay received.

While the earnings of the chief wage earner constitute the largest item in the income of the typical workingman's family, we must avoid the error too frequently made of supposing this amount to be practically synonymous with the total family income. In the case of small families, it is true that there may be no other receipts than the wages of the head of the family but, as families increase in size, it is the general rule that the income is enlarged through the efforts of the wife or children. The wife sometimes goes out as a wage-earner but, more commonly, she keeps roomers or boarders or takes in sewing or washing. The children very frequently secure work which, while generally poorly paid, aids materially in keeping the wolf from the door Besides, it must never be forgotten that a considerable minority of American skilled workers possess property the income from which is sufficient to supplement materially the wages received. Nevertheless, for the great majority of the laboring class, the height of wages in purchasing power is the fundamental determinant of economic well being.

The steady and rapid rise of the line picturing the average annual purchasing power of employees represents an epoch-making event of history. The period 1850–1900 saw that come to pass in the United States which the English economists of the earlier nineteenth century deemed impossible—the improvement of the workingman's economic welfare to the extent that he was lifted out of the conditions formerly thought inseparable from a working life. He tasted the cup of learning; he experienced the joys of leisure and entertainment; and he so limited the size of his family as to enable his children to continue to secure these advantages. Larger income and more learning naturally brought more power and secured more respect. The army of labor became an ally to be courted or any enemy to be feared.

True, a rise in the average earnings of labor does not mean that all workers participate equally therein. Many may be near the starvation border even though the masses are living in comfort. But, nevertheless, this great rise in the general income pointed to a roseate future. With American inventive genius at its height, with great stores of natural resources still but slightly drawn upon, the close of the nineteenth century gave great promise to labor of halcyon days ahead. It appeared that in this new era of prosperity, labor would command a reward so rich that it would be easy to provide for misfortune or old age. The seven hour day would give abundance of opportunity for recreation and mental culture. The high earnings would render possible the common use of many articles heretofore regarded as rare luxuries. Poverty and want would all but disappear and, under these new conditions, it was hoped that crime, too, would be greatly diminished and contentment and happiness would rule to a degree never before known to the human race. All this was portended by the unwavering rise of the purchasing power of labor.

Never before in the history of mankind had human toil been so richly rewarded—never before had the empty-handed workman been able to secure so large a return for his efforts. But accumulated wealth has always attracted the surrounding robber bands— the chance for easy winnings has invariably brought the mad rush of fortune hunters. When Rome grew rich, the Goths massed in hungry hordes along her borders gazing with greedy eyes upon her fair fields and rich cities and, at last, overpowering the defenders, the barbarians rushed over their prostrate forms and seized upon the plunder.

And so, the dawn of the twentieth century saw the spoilers gazing longingly from east and west at the riches wrested by American brawn and brains from the grasp of Nature. The advance guard of the Asiatics reached our Pacific coast but the forces of labor organized against the "Yellow Peril" and successfully repelled the invasion. But into our Atlantic ports, unresisted and almost unheeded, poured, at the same time, another army of invaders, the "White Peril" from southern and eastern Europe. And still it comes! Its advance is marked by no waving banners, no rattle of musketry, and no boom of artillery, but the army streams in company by company, regiment by regiment, brigade by brigade, and division by division. It is a peaceful army and it is composed of millions of steady, hard-working soldiers of industry. They do not ruthlessly pillage the land as did the Goths the valleys of Italy. On the other hand, they toil willingly and patiently at the hardest tasks set for them in our mines and factories. Individually, many of them are noble men and women, worthy of our highest respect, and we, who are the sons or grandsons of immigrants, should be the last, by word or deed, to cast aspersions upon the character of the new comers. Those whom we have welcomed to our shores should receive full respect and every courtesy which we would have accorded to us did we seek our fortunes in a strange land.

But, after all, the law of diminishing returns is inexorable. Every farmer's boy knows that, after a certain point is reached, doubling the work on a corn-field will not double the yield. He knows, too, that if his father were to divide his farm with two other families that it would mean hard times for all of them. And so it is with the nation as a whole. As more and more people crowd upon our soil, each one must have less and less resources with which to work, less and less help from Nature in making a living. After a certain density is reached, therefore, more population means more poverty for someone. Inventions and discoveries may postpone but they cannot avert the day of reckoning. It is not a question as to the quality of the new-comers. Granted that they are the equals in physique and character and intelligence of any of their predecessors, their arrival means that there are more mouths to share the food from the fields, more bodies to be clothed with the wool from the plains country.

And the oncoming host is made up mainly of

unskilled laborers. This means that the brunt of
the burden of their support will fall not upon the
property owner, not upon the technical expert, but
upon him who is least able to bear the load—the
common laborer of the United States. By this
invading army, then, the American workingman is
despoiled of his heritage just as surely and truly as
were the peasants of old Italy. Our priceless natural
resources must be used to feed the sons and daughters
of other lands. The marvellous inventions which
should ease the toil of the American laborer must be
utilized to their capacity to satisfy the hungry
millions of Europe. The low standard of the Old
World tends to force itself upon the New and turn
back the tide of progress.

Since 1880, the average profits of the entrepreneur,
as measured in purchasing power, have risen steadily
and rapidly. Line B in Fig. 20 shows no change in
this respect during the last decade. There has been
no great influx of foreign business men to cut the
returns for enterprise closer and closer to the borders
of starvation. Therefore, the course of profits has
been left free to respond to the great improvements in
our industrial organization resulting from American
inventive genius.

But the sixth column of Table XXXII, as illustrated by graph D in Fig. 20, shows that the American
laborer has been unable to withstand the continuous
13

onslaught of the alien hosts and that he has been forced to yield all the advantages derived from the economic progress during the decade and to content himself with a slightly lower commodity wage than he received in 1900. It is possible, however, that the seeming decline in the purchasing power of his wages is due to faulty computation of the gross wage bill of the United States or of the total number of employees. It is, therefore, advisable to compare this general result with the more detailed returns for separate fields of industry.

In manufacturing, the average annual money earnings per employee increased during the period 1899 to 1909 from $471 to $590, a rise of 25 per cent.[1] These are the Census figures and are believed to be fairly accurate. Between 1902 and 1909, the Census shows a marked decrease in the average earnings per miner. The Census of mines for 1902 was, apparently, much less accurate than the Census of manufactures of three years before. It is probable, therefore, that the reported decrease in the annual earnings was erroneous, so we shall omit these figures from consideration. The reports of the Interstate Commerce Commission show that the average annual compensation for railway employees rose from $563 in 1899 to $658 in 1909—a gain of nearly 17 per cent.[2] These

[1] *Abstract of the United States Census* for 1910, p. 438.

[2] *Statistics of Railways in the United States, 1899*, pp. 39, 49, and the *Statistical Abstract of the United States for 1912*, pp. 309-310.

figures would appear quite satisfactory were it not for the fact that the price level has been steadily climbing upward, thus lowering wages in purchasing power. While it is impossible with existing data to construct an accurate index showing the prices of goods to consumers, it is possible to obtain one, the only large error in which is almost sure to be confined to the omission of statistics of house rents. Every one knows that rents have risen in somewhat the same proportion as other commodities, so the error from this source is probably not very great. It has been necessary to use wholesale prices for part of the data, but this will not obscure the general tendencies.

The mode of computation of the index number is illustrated in Table XXXIII. The first column of this table indicates that, during the decade 1899 to 1909, the general price index rose from 99.5 to 130.0, an increase of over 30 per cent. In other words, the price level went up faster than the money earnings of labor and, hence, the real annual returns for labor showed a slight decline in the case of manufacturing and a decided decrease in the case of railway employees. And these are two of the great fields of industry.

The evidence, then, indicates that all the entrenchments of organized labor, all the legislation in favor of the working class, all of our new inventions have failed to prevent the invaders from forcing down the commodity wages of American labor.

TABLE XXXIII

INDICES OF AVERAGE PRICES OF COMMODITIES FOR THE UNITED STATES. Base 1890–1899.						
Weight.	15	9	1	3	1	1
Year.	Weighted Average of All Commodities.	Retail Food Prices.[1]	Fuel and Light.[2]	Cloths and Clothing.[3]	House Furnishing Goods.[3]	Miscellaneous.[3]
1890	105.6	101.9	105.3	113.5	111.1	110.3
1891	105.8	103.4	103.6	111.3	110.2	109.4
1892	103.7	101.6	102.2	109.0	106.5	106.2
1893	104.6	104.1	101.0	107.2	104.9	105.9
1894	98.3	99.2	93.5	96.1	100.1	99.8
1895	96.0	97.1	97.8	92.7	96.5	94.5
1896	94.6	95.2	102.9	91.3	94.0	91.4
1897	94.7	96.7	95.8	91.1	89.8	92.1
1898	97.1	99.7	94.7	93.4	92.0	92.4
1899	99.5	100.8	103.1	96.7	95.1	97.7
1900	105.3	103.0	116.0	106.8	106.1	110.5
1901	107.5	108.5	114.5	101.0	110.9	108.5
1902	112.6	114.6	127.2	102.0	112.2	112.9
1903	114.5	114.7	140.1	106.6	113.0	113.6
1904	115.0	116.2	125.5	109.8	111.7	113.0
1905	115.3	116.4	121.8	112.0	109.1	115.9
1906	120.0	120.3	124.3	120.0	111.0	122.5
1907	125.8	125.9	126.7	126.7	118.5	129.5
1908	125.4	130.1	122.8	116.9	114.0	122.8
1909	130.0	137.2	119.7	119.6	111.7	126 5
1910	135.2	144.1	117.5	123.7	111.6	131.6
1911	133.3	143.0	114.6	119.6	111.1	129.2
1912	141.0	154.2	119.1	120.7	113.7	133.6

[1] *Bulletin 140, United States Bureau of Labor Statistics*, p. 11.

[2] Estimated from *Bulletins 114 and 140 of the United States Bureau of Labor Statistics* and from the report of *The General Electric Co.*

Advocates of immigration insist that the decline in the average commodity wage of the workers of the United States in no way indicates that Americans are becoming less prosperous. On the contrary, they picture the immigrant flow as pushing itself beneath the American laborers and lifting them up to higher levels. The Americans have thus come to occupy the better positions and to receive the higher wages while the immigrant has also improved his condition over what it was in Europe. The lowered average wage may, therefore, be explained as being wholly due to an increasing share of immigrants in the total population.

This argument is so specious and subtle that a careful analysis is necessary in order to bring to light its fallacies. The first weakness of the theory lies in the fact that the diminishing average wage cannot legitimately be ascribed to an increase in the fraction of the population born in foreign lands, for the percentage of foreigners in our population was 14.7 in 1890 and still remained at the same figure in 1910, with but a slight dip in the interim. But the immigration advocate may contend that, while there has been no increase in the percentage of the foreign-born, nevertheless, the more recent arrivals are from the low-wage countries of Europe and, hence, have tended to lower the average wage, even though

[3] *Bulletin 114, United States Bureau of Labor Statistics*, p. 12. Wholesale Prices.

adding to the general prosperity of the American-born workers.

This argument, however, is a two-edged sword. If these recent-comers are from such a decidedly low-wage class, they evidently have low standards of living. We have seen that the large majority of the American working classes do not possess sufficient property to aid materially in increasing their income—to constitute any adequate recompense for a cut in their wages. In democratic America, with its free schools and broad opportunities, we cannot permanently maintain a society composed of castes and, in the next generation, if not in the present one, the descendants of the Puritans or Cavaliers will find themselves strenuously competing in the wage-market with those who trace their ancestry to Russia, Italy, or the Balkans. And, in this contest, the lowest and not the highest standard is almost sure to win.

It will be contended by some that the decline in commodity wages is due wholly to the fact that money wages have lagged behind commodity prices during the steady rise of the latter caused by our increasing money supply. This contention is worthy of careful consideration and the failure of wages in purchasing power to continue their upward trend may, partially, be accounted for in this way. We shall see later, however, that the tendency has continued for at least sixteen years, a period which would seem long enough for wages to have almost completely adjusted themselves to the rising price level. But, after all, the strongest reason for ascribing the cessation of the ascent of the purchasing power wage to immigration, lies in the fact that it would be almost inconceivable that laborers could indefinitely pour into the country without lowering wages, especially after the free land has practically disappeared. It is a well known fact that the price of labor in eastern and southern Europe is less than half what is charged for it in the United States. The free importation of any commodity from countries where it is very cheap always tends to lower the price in the importing country to that of the region from which it comes, plus freight charges. In this respect, labor is just like wheat or lumber. The shipment is not quite so easy, but, if there are no restrictions on its importation, there seems to be no possible way of avoiding the conclusion that the price must eventually be forced down to the level of the country from which the labor is sent out. And we do not even have the satisfaction of seeing the commodity value of labor in Europe greatly raised because of exports of workers to this country, for the production of labor is so rapid among the lower classes in those countries which furnish most of our immigrants that the supply is kept ever undiminished and the price always at a low level.

But, if the contention is granted that the failure of
wages, measured in purchasing power, to continue
their rise during the last decade is caused by the
increase in the labor supply offered on the markets
of the United States, why did the upward climb in
commodity wages not cease until about 1897? Immigration has been pouring across the sea for three
centuries. Is there any reason that its effects now
should differ from those of one or two generations
ago? There is this striking difference. For a century
preceding 1885, the great westward movement of the
American people was rolling across the fertile Mississippi Valley. Farms of good quality could be had
for the asking and wages could not be forced below
the amount which a man could earn by farming
this rich, moist, free land. About 1885, this great
wave reached the arid plains of the Western Highlands. It recoiled upon itself and some ten years
was occupied in filling up the interstices left unoccupied by the hasty onrush of humanity. By 1897, the
systematic forcing down of the margin had genuinely
begun, for there were no more good free lands and
more intensive cultivation became necessary in order
to supply the nation with food stuffs. Up till this
time, the flood of foreigners had poured in and been
swallowed up without serious retardation of our
progress. With this changed condition of affairs,
American labor was no longer able to avoid the attack

upon it and the enormous advantages due to the great new discoveries and inventions of the last two decades have nearly all been sacrificed in the vain endeavor to outstrip the growth of population. The immigrants have taken possession of the unskilled fields of industry, overwhelming the workers in that line, not only through actual arrivals from abroad, but through the high birth rate which furnishes a constant over-supply in the lower ranks of the laboring class. Our cities have been forced into a mushroom growth resulting in the crowding of the inhabitants into narrow and dingy quarters. All plans for city improvement have been nullified by the mad rush necessary merely to keep pace with the growing numbers. Appalled by the continuing poverty and the restless demands of the lower strata of wage earners, appeals have been made to the public to raise artificially the price of labor by establishing a legal minimum wage, all regardless of the fact that, were it effectively put into operation, it would serve merely as an added bait to draw on the waiting European multitudes.

And this is merely the economic phase of the immigration problem. The political and social evils wrought by the invading hosts are perhaps just as destructive to American welfare. Poverty, corruption, and crime are the constant camp-followers of the foreign army.[1]

[1] See *The Old World in the New*, by Professor Edward A. Ross.

Had immigration been ruthlessly shut out a generation since, there is no reason to believe that the wages of our American working class would not today be climbing steadily upward along the path marked out for them by the course of the last century. And the welfare of the workingman means the welfare of the nation, for most of the nation's population are employees and half the nation's income consists of wages and salaries.

And why has immigration been thus allowed to flow in without restriction when its injurious effects are so apparent? The reasons are two: First, the more influential class of Americans has not felt any evil effects. Cheap labor has made large profits for many great corporations, and the shareholders do not object to this. Large population has brought high rents, and landlords are well pleased. Immigration has brought travel, and the railway and steamship companies register no protests. From the standpoint, then, of the landlord, the capitalist, and the entrepreneur, no damage has been done. Only the large majority have suffered—the minority have gained or at least come through unscathed. As was noted in the last chapter, the average real income of the American people has climbed steadily upward, the census of 1910 showing no halt in the progress. If, then, wages have failed to participate in the increase, the other shares must have benefitted all the more. As was before mentioned, those members of the laboring class who own considerable property have perhaps gained more through better incomes from that source than they have lost through declining real wages. It is the practically propertyless majority who have felt the adverse effects of being compelled to compete with foreign labor.

Second: The sentimental argument has been steadily drummed into the ears of the American people by those interested in retaining a cheap labor supply.

We have had pictured to us the dire conditions of the poor Europeans and we are urged not to turn a deaf ear to their pleas, not to deny them entrance to "the land of the free." There seems no reason for granting the contention that it is the duty of Americans to remedy the poverty brought about by the ignorance and carelessness of the people of other nations. But, even were it our duty to protect the world's downtrodden, it by no means follows that we help Europe by allowing its surplus population to come freely to our shores. The immigrants are, apparently, the more energetic fraction of the lower classes of Europe. Their exit, therefore, lowers rather than raises the average quality of the people in the countries from which they come. Moreover, the lower classes in the nations that furnish the bulk of our immigration still have their numbers regulated mainly by positive checks—famine, war, disease, and starvation. The emigration of part of the population merely results in a higher birth rate and lower death rate among those remaining behind and the same overcrowding and squalor continue as before. The only recent instance in which the pressure of population has been apparently lessened at all by immigration is that of Ireland. There, the inhabitants migrated almost en masse to the United States. But a study of the population statistics of Austria, Russia, Italy, and the Balkan nations gives us no reason to believe that the emigration from those countries to the United States has materially lessened the population pressure or bettered conditions for their working people, even temporarily. Therefore, the American people suffer and Europe does not gain.

But the reader will doubtless assert that the author has been much too hasty in drawing these sweeping conclusions concerning the economical effects of immigration merely from the evidence of one admittedly doubtful estimate and of two items from government reports. In order to allay suspicions of this sort, it has been felt necessary to make a careful and rather comprehensive study of the trend of the purchasing power of wages in the United States.

According to generally accepted economic theory, the price of labor is determined by the value of its product. When labor has much capital and natural resources with which to work, the price of labor is high, and vice versa. We have seen that the capital supply has more than kept pace with the number of workers but that the land supply per man has de-

TABLE XXXIV

	INDICES OF COMMODITY PRICES AND OF HOURLY WAGES FOR MEN IN ALL INDUSTRIES. Base 1890–1899.						
Year.	Index of Money Wages.[1]	Index of Commodity Prices.	Index of Wages in Purchasing Power.	Year.	Index of Money Wages.	Index of Commodity Prices.	Index of Wages in Purchasing Power.
1850	47.1	100.6	46.8	1870	94.8	162.8	58.2
1851	47.6	111.2	42.8	1871	94.4	153.4	61.5
1852	48.8	110.4	44.2	1872	94.8	149.3	63.5
1853	49.1	118.4	41.5	1873	94.2	145.4	64.8
1854	51.4	118.4	43.4	1874	92.2	146.5	62.9
1855	52.3	123.1	42.5	1875	91.4	145.3	62.9
1856	53.1	126.6	41.9	1876	87.6	138.2	63.4
1857	54.2	128.5	42.2	1877	83.2	128.1	64.9
1858	53.0	127.6	41.6	1878	81.5	117.9	69.1
1859	53.5	116.0	46.1	1879	80.6	107.1	75.3
1860	54.2	112.7	48.1	1880	82.7	118.3	69.9
1861	54.6	106.1	51.5	1881	87.2	122.2	71.3
1862	57.2	117.4	48.8	1882	88.4	123.0	71.9
1863	65.5	149.0	44.0	1883	92.1	120.2	76.6
1864	73.9	194.0	38.1	1884	89.7	115.7	77.6
1865	82.7	261.8	31.6	1885	90.2	105.2	85.7
1866	85.8	211.6	40.6	1886	91.0	105.3	86.4
1867	90.5	186.9	48.4	1887	93.3	106.6	87.5
1868	92.7	196.1	47.3	1888	94.1	108.5	86.7
1869	94.1	171.7	54.8	1889	97.0	111.1	87.3
				1890	100.2	105.6	94.9

[1] Computed from Tables 42 and 44, *Senate Report 1394*, Part I, 1893, pp. 176–8.

TABLE XXXV

Relative Prices of Commodities and Men's Labor per Hour in All Industries.[1] Base 1890–1899.							
Year.	Labor Index.	Commodity Index.	Index of Commodity Value of Labor.	Year.	Labor Index.	Commodity Index.	Index of Commodity Value of Labor.
1890	100.2	105.6	94.8	1905	125.5	115.3	108.8
1891	100.5	105.8	95.0	1906	132.0	120.0	110.0
1892	101.8	103.7	98.1	1907	137.1	125.8	109.0
1893	101.6	104.6	97.1	1908	133.5	125.4	106.4
1894	96.7	98.3	98.4	1909	132.9	130.0	102.2
1895	98.2	96.0	102.3	1910	137.6	135.2	101.8
1896	99.0	94.6	104.7	1911	141.0	133.3	105.8
1897	99.3	94.7	104.8	1912	145.2	141.0	103.0
1898	99.6	97.1	102.6	Av. price of labor per hour, 1890–99	$0.1510		
1899	103.0	99.5	103.5				
1900	107.0	105.3	101.6				
1901	110.2	107.5	102.5				
1902	114.4	112.6	101.6	Av. price of labor per hour, 1912	$0.2192		
1903	119.8	114.5	104.6				
1904	122.6	115.0	106.6				

creased. We shall examine into the net effects which this change has produced on labor. In considering the price of labor as a commodity, each occupation and industry has been given a constant weight in order that the results might not be vitiated by a varying composition of the wage earning body at different dates. The weights are roughly proportional to the number of workers at some date chosen. The results

[1] Taken from Tables XXXIII and XXXVII.

are all computed from the reports of governmental investigations, have been carefully checked, and are believed to be reasonably accurate for the entire ground covered, except in the case of agricultural labor. This is subject to a considerable degree of error but is based on the only government reports available, those published by the Department of Agriculture.

The figures for wages preceding 1890 are all based on the Aldrich Report prepared by Roland P. Falkner. The weights there used were varied according to the reported number of workers in each industry from year to year. This gives an index of average earnings per hour rather than an index of the price of labor. The distinction is important, but it is unlikely that the difference in the weighting systems would noticeably change the indices obtained. It is almost certain that the trend of wages shown would not be materially affected.

The fact should be noted that, while we have heretofore been dealing with the earnings of all employees, the following tables take into consideration wage earners only, entirely omitting all salaried[1] workers. The first tables show changes in the hourly rates.

[1] Persons employed by the day or week are usually said to receive wages while those hired by the year are known commonly as salaried employees. The latter class includes most of the skilled clerical force, the technical experts, and managers of all sorts.

It was impossible to get accurate statistics concerning the wages of women before 1890, hence the figures for the years 1850 to 1890 are wholly for male workers.

FIGURE 21

RELATIVE PRICES OF MEN'S LABOR AND COMMODITIES, Base 1890–1899.   Continental United States.

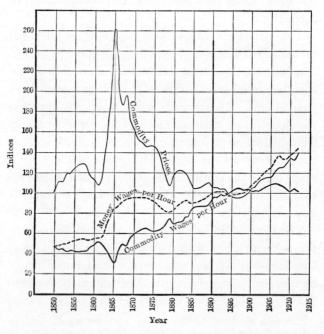

Fig. 21 illustrates the general course of the price of labor for sixty-two years. It is only necessary to call attention to a few salient features.   It is noticeable that the price of labor is much more stable than the price of other commodities. The tremendous rise of the latter in 1865, due to the greenback inflation, was accompanied by a smaller increase in money wages resulting in a marked drop in the purchasing power of an hour's work. In almost every instance, wages have failed to respond fully to short time price fluctuations and, as a result, there is close inverse correlation between the short time changes in the commodity price level and average real wages.

From 1865 to 1896, the general trend of real wages was very steadily toward higher levels, except for temporary backsets. After 1896, the progress upward ceased and, since 1906, there are some suspicious indications of a general decline. The important feature is that the ascent has been checked, and that, right in the face of the greatest industrial development that the world has ever seen. A little further vision on the part of our statesmen at Washington seems, at present, even more essential to the welfare of the working classes than does the inventive genius of the scientist in his laboratory, the monopolizing power of the labor union, or the organizing ability of the great captain of industry.

It is interesting to know whether wages have followed about the same course in different industries or whether there has been a gain in some and a loss in others; whether women's wages have kept pace with

14

those of men or whether they have risen faster or
more slowly. These points are brought out by
Tables XXXVI and XXXVII and by Fig. 22. It
is clearly seen that, in manufacturing, the wages of
men and women fluctuate together, the differences
being very slight. The relatively wide changes in
the hourly wages of miners at different periods in the

TABLE XXXVI.

RELATIVE PRICES OF COMMODITIES AND WOMEN'S LABOR
PER HOUR IN MANUFACTURING.[1]
Base 1890–1899.

Year.	Labor Index.	Commodity Index.	Index of Commodity Value of Labor.	Year.	Labor Index.	Commodity Index.	Index of Commodity Value of Labor.
1890	100.0	105.6	94.7	1905	117.6	115.3	102.0
1891	99.5	105.8	94.0	1906	125.4	120.0	104.5
1892	99.6	103.7	96.0	1907	136.7	125.8	108.6
1893	102.1	104.6	97.6	1908	135.2	125.4	107.8
1894	98.9	98.3	100.5	1909	133.5	130.0	102.6
1895	99.7	96.0	103.8	1910	137.5	135.2	101.7
1896	103.0	94.6	108.9	1911	137.7	133.3	103.3
1897	100.2	94.7	105.8	1912	147.8	141.0	104.8
1898	98.9	97.1	101.8	Av. money wage per hour, 1890–99	$0.1061		
1899	97.4	99.5	97.9				
1900	104.3	105.3	99.0				
1901	106.3	107.5	98.9	Av. money wage per hour, 1912	$0.1541		
1902	111.3	112.6	98.8				
1903	115.0	114.5	100.4				
1904	114.3	115.0	99.4				

[1] Taken from Tables XXXIII and XXXVIa.

TABLE XXXVII

INDICES[5] OF THE PRICE OF LABOR PER HOUR FOR MALE WAGE EARNERS IN VARIOUS INDUSTRIES.					
Weight.[4]	17	2	8	1	6
Year.	All Industries.	Rail-roading [1]	Manu-facturing.[2]	Mining.[6]	Agricul-ture.[3]
1890	100.2	96.3	102.1	97.0	99.4
1891	100.5	96.4	101.7	96.9	100.9
1892	101.8	99.5	101.5	109.5	101.8
1893	101.6	100.6	102.0	100.5	101.6
1894	96.7	99.4	97.2	95.5	95.4
1895	98.2	100.1	97.7	105.2	97.1
1896	99.0	100.6	98.7	99.8	98.7
1897	99.3	100.9	98.2	103.2	99.5
1898	99.6	102.5	98.9	96.6	100.2
1899	103.0	103.7	101.9	95.8	105.5
1900	107.0	105.8	105.6	99.9	110.5
1901	110.2	106.9	108.3	107.4	114.4
1902	114.4	108.5	113.1	114.7	118.1
1903	119.8	114.6	117.6	119.6	124.6
1904	122.6	118.2	116.6	135.3	130.1
1905	125.5	119.4	119.3	127.4	135.5
1906	132.0	121.3	125.6	150.4	141.0
1907	137.1	129.5	131.3	142.2	146.5
1908	133.5	132.6	127.8	127.3	142.3
1909	132.9	132.5	128.8	133.6	138.5
1910	137.6	137.5	135.1	142.4	140.2
1911	141.0	143.4	136.5	141.6	146.2
1912	145.2	145.6	140.3	149.8	150.9
Av. money price per hour, 1890–9	$0.1510	$0.1831	$0.1959	$0.2018	$0.0748
Av. 1912	.2192	.2664	.2749	.3023	.1169

[1] Estimated from the reports of the Interstate Commerce Commission.

business cycle contrast markedly with the much greater steadiness of the price of labor in manufacturing industries. It will also be noted that the gains

FIGURE 22

RELATIVE CHANGES IN THE PRICES OF COMMODITIES AND LABOR
PER HOUR IN DIFFERENT INDUSTRIES,
Base 1890–1899.   Continental United States.

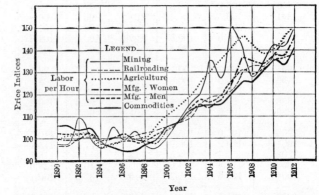

[2] Computed from the Bulletins of the United States Bureau of Labor. Weighted approximately according to the number of employees in 1900.

[3] Estimated from the Bulletin of the United States Department of Agriculture by George K. Holmes on *The Wages of Farm Labor* and from *Farmers' Bulletin 584* of the same Department. Based on wages of men hired by the year without board.

[4] Weighted approximately in proportion to the number employed in 1900.

[5] Base 1890–1899.

[6] Assumed that hours of labor varied from 9.36 in 1890 to 8.78 in 1912. Average hours of labor in 1909 given in the *United States Census for Mines and Quarries for 1909* as 8.84. See p. 31.

in the wages of agricultural labor have been slightly greater than in any other of the great fields of production.

FIGURE 23

AVERAGE PRICES OF LABOR PER HOUR IN VARIOUS
INDUSTRIES COMPARED FOR 1894–1911,
Continental United States.

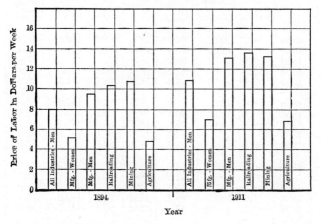

The absolute money wages per hour paid in different lines of industry are better compared by Fig. 23. The reader will observe that the disagreeable occupation of mining commands a little higher hourly wage than any of the others. The agricultural laborer receives a very low money wage for his services. This is accounted for, presumably, by the larger number of perquisites not accounted for in the records, by the lower price of commodities in the rural regions, by

TABLE XXXVIII

INDICES OF COMMODITY PRICES AND OF DAILY WAGES FOR MEN IN ALL INDUSTRIES.

Base 1890–1899.

Year.	Index of Money Wages.[1]	Index of Commodity Prices.[2]	Index of Wages in Purchasing Power.	Year.	Index of Money Wages.	Index of Commodity Prices.	Index of Wages in Purchasing Power.
1850	54.8	100.6	54.5	1870	100.7	162.8	61.9
1851	54.9	111.2	49.4	1871	100.3	153.4	65.4
1852	55.4	110.4	50.2	1872	100.7	149.3	67.5
1853	56.2	118.4	47.5	1873	100.1	145.4	68.9
1854	57.8	118.4	48.8	1874	98.0	146.5	66.9
1855	58.8	123.1	47.8	1875	95.3	145.3	65.5
1856	59.1	126.6	46.7	1876	91.3	138.2	66.0
1857	59.8	128.5	46.6	1877	86.7	128.1	67.7
1858	59.0	127.8	46.3	1878	85.0	117.9	72.0
1859	60.1	116.0	51.8	1879	84.0	107.1	78.5
1860	60.3	112.7	53.5	1880	86.2	118.3	72.9
1861	60.7	106.1	57.2	1881	90.9	122.2	74.3
1862	62.5	117.4	53.3	1882	92.2	123.0	74.9
1863	71.6	149.0	48.1	1883	96.0	120.2	79.9
1864	80.8	194.0	41.7	1884	93 5	115.7	80.8
1865	89.6	261.8	34.2	1885	94.0	105.2	89.3
1866	93.8	211.6	44.3	1886	93.9	105.3	89.2
1867	98.9	186.9	52.9	1887	94.4	106.6	88.6
1868	99.4	196.1	50.7	1888	95.2	108 5	87.8
1869	100.9	171.7	58.8	1889	98.2	111.1	88.4
				1890	101.2	105.6	95.8

[1] Adjusted to base 1890–9 from Table 42, p. 176, *Senate Report 1394, Part I, 1893.*

[2] Adjusted to base 1890–9 from Table 24, p. 93, *Senate Report 1394, Part I, 1893.*

the small degree of skill required, and by the fact that the negro population forms some thirty per cent of the entire number of agricultural laborers. Women in manufacturing receive a higher wage than that paid to men in agriculture and, yet, the women get but little more than half the pay given to men.

TABLE XXXIX

RELATIVE PRICES OF COMMODITIES AND MEN'S LABOR PER WEEK IN ALL INDUSTRIES.[1] Base 1890–1899.							
Year.	Index of Price of Labor.	Index of Commodity Prices.	Index of Commodity Value of Labor.	Year.	Index of Price of Labor.	Index of Commodity Prices.	Index of Commodity Value of Labor.
1890	101.2	105.6	95.8	1905	120.3	115.3	104.3
1891	101.9	105.8	96.3	1906	126.1	120.0	105.1
1892	103.3	103.7	99.6	1907	130.7	125.8	103.9
1893	102.2	104.6	97.7	1908	126.5	125.4	100.9
1894	96.9	98.3	98.6	1909	125.8	130.0	96.8
1895	97.8	96.0	101.8	1910	130.2	135.2	96.3
1896	98.2	94.6	103.8	1911	132.3	133.3	99.3
1897	98.2	94.7	103.7	1912	135.7	141.0	96.3
1898	98.6	97.1	101.6	Av. price of labor per week, 1890–99	$8.23		
1899	101.3	99.5	101.8				
1900	104.3	105.3	99.0				
1901	107.2	107.5	99.7				
1902	110.9	112.6	98.5	Av. price of labor per week, 1912	$11.17		
1903	115.5	114.5	100.9				
1904	117.7	115.0	102.3				

The preceding discussion has dealt with the price of labor per hour. But hours of labor change from year to year and, hence, changes in the price per day

[1] Taken from Tables XXXIII and XLI.

or week differ to some degree from the changes in the price per hour. The laborer's family is less concerned over the hourly rate than over the weekly rate, for it is the latter which largely determines the amount of commodities which may be purchased.

FIGURE 24

RELATIVE COMMODITY PRICES AND EARNINGS OF MEN,
Base 1890–1899. Continental United States.

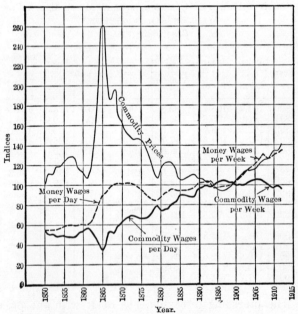

In general, there is no striking difference between the curves in Fig. 24 representing the course of weekly or daily wages and the corresponding curves for hourly wages shown in Fig. 21. The main difference lies in the fact that the hours of labor have been steadily shortened with the result that daily or weekly wages rose more slowly before 1896 than did hourly wages and, since that date, have declined to a noticeably greater extent than the latter. The wages of men and women, while not fluctuating together at all times, have, in general, shown like tendencies.

During the last fifteen years, the rising money wages have served to hide from the workingman the fact that the shortening of his hours of labor was resulting in a decrease in the power of his daily earnings to buy the commodities desired.

Table XL indicates a decline of over 10 per cent in the weekly wages in purchasing power of women since 1896 as against a fall of 8 per cent in the commodity wages of men since the same date. These indices are all computed on the basis of full time weekly earnings and show nothing concerning loss of time or overtime. While the extent of employment fluctuates steadily with the business cycle, there is no evidence to show that, in the long run, it is becoming of either greater or less importance than formerly.

Table XLI compares weekly wages by industries. The absolute payments in the various industries in 1894 and 1911 are illustrated in Fig. 25. It will be observed that the changes occurring are, relatively, considerably less than those taking place in hourly wages during the same seventeen year interval.

Much stress has been laid in the preceding pages upon the fact that the purchasing power of wages has

TABLE XL

RELATIVE PRICES OF COMMODITIES AND WOMEN'S[1] LABOR PER WEEK IN MANUFACTURING. Base 1890–1899.							
Year.	Labor Index.[2]	Commodity Index.	Index of Commodity Value of Labor.	Year.	Labor Index.	Commodity Index.	Index of Commodity Value of Labor.
1890	101.0	105.6	95.6	1905	115.7	115.3	100.3
1891	100.9	105.8	95.4	1906	122.9	120.0	102.4
1892	101.0	103.7	97.4	1907	133.0	125.8	105.7
1893	102.1	104.6	97.6	1908	130.6	125.4	104.1
1894	96.4	98.3	98.1	1909	129.0	130.0	99.2
1895	99.6	96.0	103.7	1910	130.7	135.2	96.7
1896	102.7	94.6	108.6	1911	130.9	133.3	98.2
1897	99.7	94.7	105.2	1912	138.3	141.0	98.1
1898	99.1	97.1	102.1	Av. money wage per week, 1890–99	$5.33[3]		
1899	97.5	99.5	98.0				
1900	103.9	105.3	98.7				
1901	105.8	107.5	98.4	Av. money wage per week, 1912	$7.38[3]		
1902	110.3	112.6	97.9				
1903	113.4	114.5	99.0				
1904	112.3	115.0	97.6				

[1] Women sixteen years of age and over.

[2] Computed from *Bulletins 128 and 134 of the United States Bureau of Labor Statistics*.

[3] Estimated from Part IV, p. 645, *United States Census of Manufactures for 1905*.

TABLE XLI

INDICES OF THE PRICE OF LABOR PER WEEK FOR MALE WAGE EARNERS IN VARIOUS INDUSTRIES.					
Weight.[5]	17	2	8	1	6
Year.	All Industries.	Railroading.[1]	Manufacturing.[2]	Mining.[3]	Agriculture.[4]
1890	101.2	99.1	103.0	98.3	101.5
1891	101.9	98.7	102.4	97.7	103.0
1892	103.3	101.4	102.2	110.3	104.4
1893	102.2	102.0	102.1	100.9	102.8
1894	96.9	99.3	97.6	95.6	95.6
1895	97.8	99.4	97.7	105.1	96.4
1896	98.2	99.5	98.6	99.3	97.1
1897	98.2	99.3	97.6	102.5	97.9
1898	98.6	100.3	98.6	95.6	98.6
1899	101.3	100.9	101.2	94.6	102.7
1900	104.3	102.4	104.1	98.3	106.4
1901	107.2	102.9	106.5	105.1	110.1
1902	110.9	104.4	110.4	111.4	113.9
1903	115.5	109.1	114.2	116.7	119.2
1904	117.7	112.0	112.4	131.9	124.4
1905	120.3	112.5	115.0	124.0	129.6
1906	126.1	113.6	120.4	145.5	134.7
1907	130.7	120 6	125.5	137.2	140.0
1908	126.5	122.8	122.2	122.4	134.4
1909	125.8	122.1	122.6	127.7	131.0
1910	130.2	125.8	127.9	136.1	133.8
1911	132.3	130.5	128.7	135.0	137.6
1912	135.7	132.3	131.7	142.4	141.2
Av. money price per week, 1890–1899	$ 8.23	$10.44[7]	$ 9.70[6]	$11.31[8]	$5.02
Av. 1912	$11.17	13.81	12.77[6]	15.93[8]	7.09

[1] Estimated from the reports of the Interstate Commerce Commission.

FIGURE 25

AVERAGE PRICES OF LABOR PER WEEK IN VARIOUS INDUS-
TRIES COMPARED FOR 1894–1911,
Continental United States.

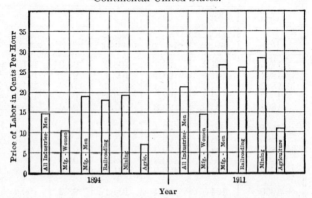

[2] Computed from the bulletins of the United States Bureau of
Labor.

[3] Estimated from the *Aldrich Report, Part IV*, p. 1567, from the
Second Annual Report of the United States Commissioner of Labor,
and from the *Reports of the Bureaus of Labor of Pennsylvania,
West Virginia and Ohio.*

[4] Estimated from the bulletin of the United States Department
of Agriculture for 1910 written by George K. Holmes on *The
Wages of Farm Labor;* also from *Farmer's Bulletin 584* of the same
Department.

[5] Weighted approximately according to the number of males
employed in 1900.

[6] Estimated on the basis of the figures given in the *Census of
Manufactures for 1905, Part IV*, p. 645.

[7] Estimated on a basis of an average of 57 hours per week in
the base decade.

[8] Computed on the basis of the *United States Census of Mines
and Quarries for 1902*, p. 99.

remained stationary or declined slightly during the last sixteen years. But it must not be inferred from this that the present condition of the American laboring class is bad as compared to that of the working classes elsewhere. On the contrary, the workingman in this country is far more prosperous than in most nations of the globe. We have seen that, in 1912, his average wage in all industries was approximately $11 per week. If we figure his average annual employment as 49 weeks, he is paid in the neighborhood of $547 per year,[1] by no means a princely sum but more than double the amount earned by a European workman and probably four times what the laborer of China, Japan, or India can hope to receive. When we remember that this is supplemented, in a very large percentage of cases, by earnings of the wife or children or by income from property, the income of the average American working family can not be considered niggardly. Education has intensified the worker's feeling of dissatisfaction with the environment by which he must often, perforce, be surrounded but it has, at the same time, sharpened his appreciative faculties, thus increasing the amount of real income derived from a given unit of expenditure. The advent of the motion picture has furnished an exten-

[1] This accords fairly well with the estimate of Scott Nearing in *Wages in the United States*, p. 208, in which he places the average annual earnings of an adult male worker in the northeast quarter of the United States at $600.

sive field of enjoyment at comparatively slight expense. Other consumers beside the working class have been compelled to share in the expense of compensating unfortunate workers for time lost because of accidents. The decline in the purchasing power of wages has also been offset by an increased income from public sources. Better streets and lights, better hospitals, better libraries, better parks and playgrounds, and better schools have all enhanced the real income of the common people, and the tax-burden of the ordinary laborer for these purposes is comparatively light.

But this does not gainsay the fact that the lot of the unskilled laborer, who must meet the competition of the new arrival from abroad, is a hard one, and, what is much worse, that there is, under present circumstances, no hope of bettering his condition but rather a probability that it will steadily grow more unbearable unless he is protected from the competition of the ill-paid workers of Europe. Furthermore, the skilled American workman is sure, sooner or later, to feel the sympathetic downward pull caused by low wages in unskilled trades. Always, the children of the unskilled will seek, with some success, to enter his trade and cut the wages below what he believes to be necessary for a decent existence. And it is highly improbable that union walls, no matter how strongly built, can withstand for long the constant battering carried on by the low-paid throng without. For generations, we have dallied with the useless attempt to keep up the price of labor by protecting commodities against foreign competition, all unmindful of the teachings of economists that labor could not be protected by duties on goods. Meanwhile, our statesmen have ignored and continue to ignore the rather simple truth that the "real" wage of labor can be kept up only by protecting our workingmen directly against foreign importations of labor. Without such safeguards, there seems to be no reason to suppose that we can prevent the wage level in the United States from settling gradually down to that of Europe. This would mean a ruthless cut in wages all along the line with a consequent breaking down of our present high standards of living and the forcing down of unskilled labor to a mere subsistence level, thus, for this country, turning back a century or more the hands of progress. Against the continuance of such a ruinous policy, it has become the duty of every patriotic American to register a vigorous protest.

CHAPTER VIII

THE SHARE OF THE CORPORATION IN THE TOTAL NATIONAL PRODUCT

ONE of the striking features of the evolution of modern industrial society has been the development of the corporation. The only statistics in this field are of such very recent origin that, except for the last few years, no quantitative study of the growth of this form of organization can be presented which can lay any claim to accuracy. From the United States Census, we find that, during the decade 1899–1909, the fraction of the mineral output produced by corporation owned mines increased from about 85.0 to 92.2 per cent, while, in the manufacturing field, during the same period, corporations increased their share of the value added by manufactures from approximately 63.3 to 77.2 per cent. We know that transportation by water, rail, and wire has been mainly carried on by corporations for several decades. In commercial enterprises, the general impression is that the stock company is gradually playing a more important part than formerly. Only in the field of agriculture, does the individual entrepreneur—the man who controls and directs his own business—still remain dominant and almost without corporate rivals. A rough estimate indicates that, of the total products of American industry in 1899, some 39 per cent, or approximately seven billion dollars' worth, and, in 1909, about 44 per cent, or thirteen billion dollars' worth, were turned out by corporation-owned plants.

Since the date of the Thirteenth Census, the evidence points to a continuous growth of corporation activity. According to the estimates of dividends and interest payments given monthly by the *New York Journal of Commerce*, dividends paid by the larger corporations have increased from six hundred and twelve millions in 1909, to eight hundred and eight millions of dollars in 1913, and the first seven months of 1914 show an increase of nearly four per cent over the same period for the preceding year.

Interest payments made by corporations seem to be advancing at even a more rapid rate, having risen from seven hundred and sixty three million dollars in 1911 to nine hundred and thirteen million dollars in 1913, and the disbursements for 1914 are, apparently, nearly seven per cent greater than those for 1913.

The total net income of the corporations of the United States, according to the returns made to the revenue authorities, amounted, in 1912, to $3,213,707,247. This does not include interest paid on indebtedness but it is a generally admitted fact

15

that the bond holder is merely a privileged participant in the earnings of the corporation.   Thus, to ascertain the share of the national income distributed to the public through corporate agencies, we must add in the interest on debts.   A considerable part of the net revenue of every well managed corporation is used in building up the physical plant of the company, in increasing the working capital or in providing for emergencies.   If we allow that 30 per cent of the entire income available for dividends is put into improvements, we should get a total dividend disbursement for 1912 of $2,249,300,000.   The corporations whose payments are reported for 1912 by the *New York Journal of Commerce* paid out $1.09 in interest for every dollar of dividends.   If we assume this same rate to hold for all corporations in the United States, their total payments to investors amounted, in 1912, to about $4,700,000,000.

By combining these rough estimates with others of a like nature, we obtain the following table which is, of course, far from accurate but which, nevertheless, is a good enough approximation to illustrate some of the principal features of corporation growth.

The main conclusions which may be safely drawn from Table XLII are: first, that the corporation is a very important factor in the productive forces of the nation; and, second, that the amount of the products which it succeeds in retaining and distributing to the investors in corporation securities forms a significant and constantly increasing fraction of the total national income. Under these circumstances, it is not surprising that questions of corporation control have played so important a part in the political life of the United States for the last quarter century.

TABLE XLII

ESTIMATED RECENT CHANGES IN CORPORATE INCOMES.						
Year.	Value of Corporation Products in Millions of Dollars.	Percentage of National Dividend Produced in Corporation Owned Plants.	Payments in Millions of Dollars by Corporations to Investors.			Percentage of Total National Dividend Paid by Corporations to Investors.
			Total.	Interest.	Dividends.	
1899	7,034	39.2	2,220	1,200	1,020	12.3
1909	13,351	43.7	4,214	2,341	1,873	13.8
1912			4,699	2,450	2,249	
1914			4,781	2,620	2,161	

The corporate form of organization has been both lauded and condemned. Its friends have maintained that it furnishes the ideal method of suiting the convenience of investors. Through corporate organization, it is possible to provide securities adapted to the most conservative or to the most speculative investor. Furthermore, the man with one hundred or the man with one million dollars can be equally well accommodated. The stocks and bonds can be distributed among tens of thousands of holders and yet the centralization of management in a small board of directors gives a high degree of efficiency in carrying on its business. In fact, its proponents have been so favorably impressed with this simple method of control that they have, with considerable success, advocated its adoption as the one ideal form of city government and, as a result, we see commission governed cities on all sides.

Indeed, in the opinion of some learned men, the corporation furnishes the key to the solution of other great social and political issues. The monopoly problem disappears when the stock becomes widely enough distributed, for, then, any exorbitant gains will be scattered among the masses of the people as dividends and so the general public will be as well off as if the monopoly charged low prices and secured reasonable profits only. Likewise, the labor problem will vanish when the laborers become the stockholders of the corporations by which they are employed. If the corporation should set wages too low, dividends will be that much larger and the employee-stock-holders will gain in one way what they lose in another. If the hours or conditions of employment are unsatisfactory, the workmen can complain against themselves but, if they strike, they will lose both wages and dividends, hence, no such disturbances of industry will occur. And, in a similar manner, the good features of the corporation may be set forth indefinitely.

On the other hand, the rabid corporation-baiter denounces the stock company as a thing without a soul whose principal function appears to be to prey upon the public and to override the wishes of the people as expressed in law.

As in most controversies, there is a measure of truth in the arguments of each side. It is only recently coming to be realized, however, that the problems of the corporation are largely the problems of republican government in general. The old-time corporation with a dozen members has little more resemblance to the great modern "octopus" with a hundred thousand share-holders than does the town meeting to the American Republic.

It has only been in recent years that the American people have come generally to invest their savings in the securities of the great railways or industrial concerns. The result has been a tremendous increase in the number of stockholders, a surprisingly large share of the smaller investors being women.

The small stockholder has far less voice in the management of the corporation than he has in controlling the state government. He receives no enlightenment concerning the policies of candidates for the Board of Directors. No opportunity is given him to cast an intelligent ballot unless he happens to be in a position to attend the annual meeting, something which is, of course, extremely

unusual. As a result, he contributes his funds and
then trusts to the good faith of directors over whom
he has no control whatever, to treat him fairly in the
distribution of profits. In many cases, boards of
directors have dealt justly with the small stockholders; in too numerous instances, they have, by
skillful manipulations, turned everything above minimum gains into their own pockets or into the coffers
of the controlling stockholders. And, very rarely
indeed, have they been punished or even compelled
to return the loot.

Recent exposures have caused a general demand
that this condition of affairs be remedied, but to
find adequate means of so doing has not proved easy.
In fact, the difficulties in the way of securing responsi-
bility of the directors to the minor stockholders
while, at the same time, insuring that the business
will be efficiently conducted, seem remarkably similar
to those involved in the establishment of a successful
socialistic state, the query in the latter instance
being: "How is it possible to secure efficiency in
administration while still retaining adequate control
for the people?" For, after all, the great corporation
very closely resembles a state. It is a coöperative
undertaking in which many thousands unite for a
common benefit and delegate their interests to a
central government. This central governing body
may, in either case, use its power for the good of the

people whom it represents or it may selfishly seize the
opportunity to enrich itself at the public expense.
The directorate may make war on rival corporations
while the governing power of a nation may declare
war on other states. The directors, like the legis-
lators or administrators, may be honest or dishonest,
efficient or inefficient. In fact, the parallel is so
close that it seems more than probable that whoever
discovers the secret of combining efficiency in administration and effective control by the stockholders of a
corporation will, at the same time, have brought to
light the most satisfactory and economical system of
administering industry under government ownership.

It is a well known fact that, during the last half
century, the tendency has been for industry to become
more and more concentrated and integrated. Most
people believe that there are immense economies
which can be effected only by very large scale combinations, and many are confident that monopoly is,
as a rule, the most economical of all forms of control.
Some maintain, however, that monopoly, by its
carelessness, sacrifices more than it gains through the
elimination of the wastes of competition.

What, then, is the destiny toward which our
industrial organization is tending? Will competition
be revived, strengthened, and rehabilitated by the
imposition of legal restraint upon monopolistic
activities? On the other hand, will the present

tendency for corporations to control a larger and larger fraction of our industry continue until the individual entrepreneur becomes a rarity? Will these giant monopolistic corporations, owned perhaps by the workers in the industry, control whole sections of the industrial field? Shall we see the sugar industry, operated as one tremendous unit in which all persons interested in the sugar business are firmly united, engage in terrific economic combats with the similarly closely knit steel trust or wheat combine? Will these great monopolies overshadow our present governments based on geographic units so that we shall all owe allegiance to an industry rather than to a state? Or shall we, instead, see the present tendency to the extension of governmental activities continue until all industries are owned and operated by the state or nation and the corporation must needs disappear for lack of activities in which to engage? Or, shall we continue to have the present mixture of monopoly and competition, of individual, corporate, and governmental control of industry? These questions furnish an interesting field for speculation but interpretations of present tendencies will differ widely according to the beliefs and predilections of the person studying the problem.

CHAPTER IX

THE DISTRIBUTION OF INCOME AMONG FAMILIES

THE last two chapters covered, in a general way, the distribution of income among industries and factors of production. In this chapter, the attempt will first be made to classify roughly the twenty-eight millions of families living in the Continental United States according to the income which each, respectively, receives. And this is a most important classification for, indeed, of all tests, income is the best single criterion of economic welfare. Wealth is a better safeguard against disaster. It sometimes is a more effective source of power. But, in every day experience, no other quest is carried on so assiduously as that for the maximum income. Income will obtain the necessities, comforts and luxuries of life. It will, if saved, lead to the added advantages of wealth. It is worth while, then, to know who gets the thirty billions of book income annually distributed among the people of the United States.

THE INCOME SHARES OF THE VARIOUS CLASSES

Unfortunately, it has not been found possible to make a satisfactory historical investigation of this topic. It is, however, probable that something may

be inferred from a study of Fig. 19 as to the changes
in the relative distribution which have taken place.
It seems almost certain that a fall in the share of
wages means a lessening in the proportion of the total
income received by the working classes and vice versa,
for the fraction of the income of working people
obtained from other sources is relatively so small that
changes therein would hardly offset fluctuations in
the wage share.   If this assumption is true, the fraction of the total income going to the favored few
decreased during the period 1850 to 1890, but, since
that date, has been on the increase. We would
expect that the freeing of the slaves and the breaking
up of the plantations after the Civil War would result
in a much more equal distribution of income.   The
settlement of the Mississippi Valley, with the resulting
multiplication of valuable farm buildings, would
have a similar effect.   On the other hand, the recent
growth of the great class who seem destined to remain
lifelong wage-workers in the employ of mammoth
industrial concerns, would tend toward less uniform
distribution.   But the greatest force in the last three
decades making for income concentration has been
the successful organization of monster corporations.
The promoters and manipulators of these concerns
have received, as their share of the spoils, permanent
income claims, in the shape of securities, large enough
to make Crœsus appear like a pauper.

Thus, while the belief must at present remain without positive verification, there is considerable evidence to indicate that a larger fraction of the income is now concentrated in the hands of a few of the very rich, than was the case twenty years ago. The marked stability shown by the distribution of wealth during the preceding seventy years makes us doubt, however, that the shift in the relative shares of income held by the different fractions of the population has been so great as to be at all startling.

The only serious attempt in recent years to study the distribution of incomes in the United States is that admirable compilation and analysis of sources made by Frank H. Streightoff and published under the title " *The Distribution of Incomes in the United States,*" as Number 2, in the 1912 volume of " *The Columbia University Studies.*" [1] In this monograph, Mr. Streightoff asserts that it is, at present, impossible to give any accurate picture of the distribution of incomes among the population as a whole. The present writer is heartily in accord with this statement. True, the data from the Wisconsin income tax compiled by Professor Henry M. Trumbower of the University of Wisconsin, have yielded much valuable information not available to Mr. Streightoff,

[1] The reader is referred to this work for much valuable source material and for a decidedly good bibliography.

but even these figures are subject to the error common
to all statistics, derived from assessment reports, of
having incomes reported below the actual amounts.
A more serious weakness lies in the fact that the
Wisconsin data fail to cover satisfactorily the incomes
below $1800 and these lower incomes apply to the
great mass of the population. Nevertheless, these
statistics have aided immensely by giving an inkling
concerning the shape of the distribution curve for
the incomes of the middle class and above. Wisconsin, too, is a peculiarly good sample state for it con-
tains one large city, many smaller cities and villages,
and much agricultural territory. Its per capita
wealth is about equal to the average for the United
States as a whole.   It is located neither in the richest
nor the poorest section of the country. Under the
circumstances, the error should not be very great in
considering the central part of the curve for Wisconsin as fairly representative for the middle class
throughout the entire nation and that is the course
which has been adopted in making the estimates
which follow.

The United States Treasury Department and
various Congressional committees have estimated
the incomes of the very rich in a few of the metropolitan cities of the East. Only preliminary reports
from the National income tax are as yet available
but these give us some information concerning the

incomes of that very small section of the people who control a large fraction of the country's wealth.

Rather abundant material can be found dealing with the distribution of income among wage earners, but studies of the income of the high salaried classes and of the entrepreneurs are rare indeed. Under the first head, we have the investigations of the Bureaus of Labor of the United States. These have given us much information concerning the distribution of wages, and even of incomes, among the families of working men. They have been supplemented by such private studies as those of Chapin[1] and More[2] for the City of New York.

In compiling the data which follow, the sources cited above, together with the United States Census and numerous private studies, were utilized to a greater or lesser extent. The methods followed in combining the figures were mainly graphic and were too varied to describe here. Full allowances were made for the changes in wages occurring between the respective dates to which the studies applied and 1910, for the earnings of other members of the family, for income from investments, and for unemployment. While the corrections were in no case entirely accurate, yet, they are all based upon the results of careful investigations. For example, the trend of wages was

[1] Chapin, Robert Coit, *The Standard of Living Among Workingmen's Families in New York City.*

[2] More, Mrs. Louise Boland, *Wage-Earner's Budgets.*

taken from the study shown in Tables XXXVIII and XXXIX; unemployment was corrected by the use of figures taken from the United States Census of Occupations. Earnings from the other sources than labor were estimated from the studies recorded in the *Eighteenth Annual Report of the United States Commissioner of Labor*. No pretense is made that the final figures are accurate but they will, at least, serve as a starting point for more detailed studies. Much time has been spent in collecting and adjusting data and in reducing all errors to a minimum. The success which has attended these efforts must, for the present, remain more or less problematical. When Mr. Streightoff wrote, he was correct in asserting that the material was insufficient to permit of any general estimate of the distribution of income among all American families and the truth must be recognized that any accurate tabulation of results is still impossible. But, despite unavoidable errors, due to the paucity of the material available, it is believed that, in its larger aspects, the distribution set forth in Table XLIII and Figs. 26 and 27, does not vary widely from the truth.

Any classification of income must, necessarily, be based upon receipts of families rather than individuals for it is by families that incomes are received and disbursed. The head of the family ordinarily divides income between himself and his various dependents in the proportions that he deems best. The family, then, acts as a unit. Some families consist of only one person. This is true in the case of an unmarried man or woman who is self-supporting and yet has no dependents. A larger number of families consist of a husband with his wife, children, and perhaps dependent relatives or a widow with her children.

But a moment's consideration will show us that a given family income, by no means, denotes a uniform standard of prosperity. This is especially true because of the different numbers dependent thereon for support. A single man or woman may receive only six hundred dollars a year and yet maintain a rather high standard of living while a married man with six children may find it difficult to keep his family in decency though he receives a salary of twelve hundred dollars per annum. This shows the desirability of classifying families according to their size as well as according to their income.

It was found feasible to divide the families of the United States receiving $1,400 or less into three classes—viz., independent single men, independent single women, and families with dependents. For families with larger incomes, this separation was not made but it may be remarked that, among the higher income classes, the single men and women are, relatively, much less numerous than in the very low income groups.

TABLE XLIII

THE ESTIMATED[1] DISTRIBUTION OF INCOME AMONG THE FAMILIES OF THE CONTINENTAL UNITED STATES IN 1910.[3]

Family Income.	Number of Income Receiving Units in Thousands.				Total Income of Class in Millions of Dollars.	Cumulative[2] Number of Income Receiving Units in Thousands.	Cumulative Amount of Income in Millions of Dollars.
	Single Men.	Single Women.	Men or Widows with Families.	Total.			
$ 0–$200	10	10	0	20	3	20	3
200– 300	150	70	50	270	72	290	75
300– 400	853	560	300	1,713	625	2,003	700
400– 500	1,575	530	560	2,665	1,239	4,668	1,939
500– 600	1,380	280	960	2,620	1,480	7,288	3,419
600– 700	970	150	2,470	3,590	2,388	10,878	5,807
700– 800	715	110	2,700	3,525	2,697	14,403	8,504
800– 900	600	37	2,100	2,737	2,327	17,140	10,831
900–1000	600	22	1,640	2,262	2,138	19,402	12,969
1000–1100	410	16	1,400	1,826	1,908	21,228	14,877
1100–1200	290	12	1,300	1,602	1,826	22,830	16,703
1200–1300	200	8	1,020	1,228	1,523	24,058	18,226
1300–1400	105	5	600	710	955	24,768	19,181

[1] Principal sources used in compiling this table:

Trumbower, Henry M., Manuscript study of *The Distribution of Income in Wisconsin.*

Eighteenth Annual Report of the United States Commissioner of Labor.

Estimates by the Treasury Department for the Ways and Means Committee of the House of Representatives. April 22, 1913.

United States Census Reports:—Mining 1902. Manufacturing, 1900; 1905. Electric Railways, 1907. Bulletins, 93; 94; Census of 1900.

Wage Statistics of the City of Chicago, 1902, App. A.

Report of the Superintendent of Public Instruction for Michigan, 1910.

Report of the Methodist Conference for 1910.

TABLE XLIII (Cont.)

THE ESTIMATED DISTRIBUTION OF INCOME AMONG THE
FAMILIES OF THE CONTINENTAL UNITED STATES IN 1910.

Family Income in Thousands of Dollars.	Number of Families.	Total Income of Class in Millions of Dollars.	Cumulative Number of Families.	Cumulative Amount of Income in Millions of Dollars.
1.4– 1.5	475,000	686	25,243,000	19,867
1.5– 1.6	385,000	595	25,628,000	20,462
1.6– 1.7	306,000	503	25,934,000	20,965
1.7– 1.8	243,000	423	26,177,000	21,388
1.8– 1.9	189,000	348	26,366,000	21,736
1.9– 2.0	142,000	275	26,508,000	22,011
2.0– 2.2	200,000	416	26,708,000	22,427
2.2– 2.4	167,000	381	26,875,000	22,808
2.4– 2.6	141,000	350	27,016,000	23,158
2.6– 2.8	115,000	308	27,131,000	23,466
2.8– 3.0	94,000	271	27,225,000	23,737
3.0– 3.2	77,000	237	27,302,000	23,974
3.2– 3.4	63,000	207	27,365,000	24,181
3.4– 3.6	52,000	181	27,417,000	24,362
3.6– 3.8	43,000	158	27,460,000	24,520
3.8– 4.0	36,000	140	27,496,000	24,660
4.0– 4.4	59,000	245	27,555,000	24,905
4.4– 4.8	49,000	223	27,604,000	25,128
4.8– 5.2	40,000	198	27,644,000	25,326
5.2– 5.6	32,000	172	27,676,000	25,498
5.6– 6.0	25,000	144	27,701,000	25,642
6.0– 7.0	46,000	294	27,747,000	25,936
7.0– 8.0	33,000	244	27,780,000	26,180
8.0– 10.0	38,000	334	27,818,000	26,514
10.0– 12.0	22,000	238	27,840,000	26,752
12.0– 16.0	31,000	425	27,871,000	27,177
16.0– 20.0	20,000	354	27,891,000	27,531
20.0– 30.0	20,000	480	27,911,000	28,011
30.0– 40.0	12,000	408	27,923,000	28,419
40.0– 50.0	7,000	308	27,930,000	28,727
50.0–100.0	11,630	794	27,941,630	29,521
100.0–200.0	3,145	391	27,944,775	29,912

16

TABLE XLIII (Cont.)

THE ESTIMATED[1] DISTRIBUTION OF INCOME AMONG THE FAMILIES OF THE CONTINENTAL UNITED STATES IN 1910.[3]				
Family Income in Thousands of Dollars.	Number of Families.	Total Income of Class in Millions of Dollars.	Cumulative[2] Number of Families.	Cumulative Amount of Income in Millions of Dollars.
200– 1,000	261	126	27,945,036	30,038
1,000– 2,000	98	136	27,945,134	30,174
2,000– 5,000	41	118	27,945,175	30,292
5,000–10,000	10	79	27,945,185	30,371
10,000–50,000	5	158	27,945,190	30,529

It is, perhaps, worth while to compare the income distribution, as estimated in Table XLIV, with the figures computed in 1896 by Dr. Charles B. Spahr.[4]

[1] Continued—.

Statistical Abstract of the United States, 1911.

Bulletin 295, Cornell University.

Senate Document 380; Vol. 5, p. 645.

[2] See note to Table X.

[3] Preliminary reports from the returns of the United States income tax, as cited in *The Commercial and Financial Chronicle* for October 24, 1914, indicate that the above estimates show decidedly too many families with very large incomes. The authorities of the Treasury Department believe, however, that there have been wholesale evasions of the tax by the richer classes and there are strong indications that this view is correct. While the inequality in income distribution is, therefore, probably somewhat less than indicated by this table, it is still too early to decide that any radical revision is necessary in order to accord with the facts. The changes in the Lorenz curve, corresponding with estimates based on the Income Tax of 1913, are shown in Figs. 26 and 27.

[4] *The Present Distribution of Wealth in the United States*, p. 128.

According to his table, 88 per cent of the people received annually less than $1,200 while our present estimate puts 82 per cent of the families in that class. He calculated that 1.6 per cent of the wealthiest

FIGURE 26

A COMPARISON BY LORENZ CURVES OF THE DISTRIBUTION OF INCOME IN THE UNITED STATES AND PRUSSIA WITH THE DISTRIBUTION OF WEALTH IN WISCONSIN, PRUSSIA, FRANCE, AND THE UNITED KINGDOM.

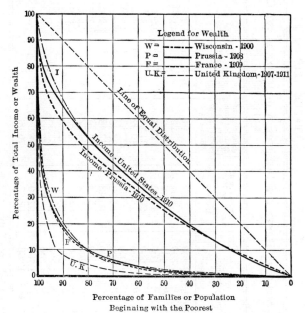

I. Distribution of Income indicated by U. S. Income Tax Returns, 1913.

TABLE XLIV

THE ESTIMATED PERCENTAGE DISTRIBUTION OF INCOME IN THE CONTINENTAL UNITED STATES IN 1910.[1]

Family Income.	Percentage of Families Having Given Income.	Percentage of Total Income Received by Given Class of Families.	Family Income.	Percentage of Families Having Given Income.	Percentage of Total Income Received by Given Class of Families.
Less than $ 200	.07	.01	Less than 1,900	94.34	71.20
" " 300	1.04	.25	" " 2,000	94.86	72.10
" " 400	7.17	2.29			
" " 500	16.70	6.35	" " 2,200	95.58	73.46
" " 600	26.08	11.20	" " 2,400	96.18	74.71
" " 700	38.92	19.02	" " 2,600	96.67	75.86
" " 800	51.54	27.86	" " 2,800	97.08	76.86
" " 900	61.33	35.48	" " 3,000	97.42	77.76
" " 1,000	69.43	42.48	" " 3,200	97.70	78.54
" " 1,100	75.96	48.73	" " 3,400	97.92	79.21
" " 1,200	81.69	54.72	" " 3,600	98.10	79.81
" " 1,300	86.08	59.70	" " 3,800	98.26	80.32
" " 1,400	88.62	62.83	" " 4,000	98.39	80.78
" " 1,500	90.31	65.08			
" " 1,600	91.70	67.03			
" " 1,700	92.80	68.68			
" " 1,800	93.67	70.06			

[1] Computed from Table XLIII.

TABLE XLIV (Cont.)

The Estimated Percentage Distribution of Income in the Continental United States in 1910.

Family Income in Thousands of Dollars	Percentage of Families Having Given Income.	Percentage of Total Income Received by Given Class of Families.	Family Income in Thousands of Dollars	Percentage of Families Having Given Income.	Percentage of Total Income Received by Given Class of Families.
Less than 4.4	98.60	81.58	Less than 100.0	99.98726	96.70
" 4.8	98.78	82.31	" 200.0	99.99851	97.98
" 5.2	98.92	82.96	" 1,000.0	99.99945	98.39
" 5.6	99.03	83.52	" 2,000.0	99.99980	98.84
" 6.0	99.12	84.00	" 5,000.0	99.99994	99.24
" 7.0	99.29	84.95	" 10,000.0	99.99998	99.49
" 8.0	99.41	85.76	" 50,000.0	100.00000	100.00
" 10.0	99.54	86.86			
" 12.0	99.62	87.64			
" 16.0	99.74	89.02			
" 20.0	99.81	90.18			
" 30.0	99.88	91.76			
" 40.0	99.92	93.09			
" 50.0	99.94	94.10			

received over $5,000, while the figures in Table XLIV show only 1.2 per cent above that line.

A COMPARISON BY LORENZ CURVES OF THE DISTRIBUTION OF INCOME AMONG THE RICHEST FAMILIES IN THE UNITED STATES AND PRUSSIA.

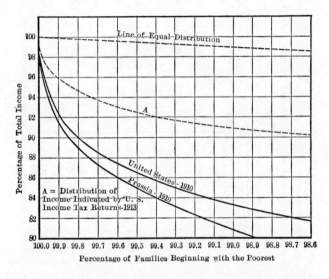

Percentage of Families Beginning with the Poorest

If the figures are placed on a percentage basis, in order that they may be compared with Fig. 26, Dr. Spahr's calculation would show 88 per cent of the people receiving 65 per cent of the income in 1896. The present writer's estimate for 1910 would make

the same percentage of the population absorb about
62 per cent of the income stream. Dr. Spahr believed
that 1.6 per cent of the richest families secured 10.8
per cent of the income while Fig. 27 would indicate
that the same fraction of the population now controls
some 19 per cent of the income

If all the estimates cited are correct, it indicates
that, since 1896, there has occurred a marked concentration of income in the hands of the very rich;
that the poor have, relatively, lost but little; but that
the middle class has been the principal sufferer.
This evidence of increasing concentration would
accord with the inference drawn from the decreasing
share of the product going to wages, which was discussed in the early part of this chapter.

One of the most striking things brought out by the
Lorenz curves in Fig. 26 is the marked way in which
the distribution of wealth and income differ, the
inequality, in the case of income, being very decidedly
less than in the case of wealth. For instance, the
poorest half of the people of Wisconsin own but two
or three per cent of the wealth but they receive more
than one-fourth of the income.

From Fig. 27, we see that the richest one per cent
of the Prussian people own only 19 per cent of the
income while Fig. 9 showed that they possessed about
49 per cent of the wealth. For the United States,
the same graphs indicate that the richest hundredth

of the people possess approximately 15 per cent of the income and 47 per cent of the wealth. Whether, then, we consider one extreme or the other, we observe the fact that income is far more equally participated in than wealth. But this is what one might expect, after all. The working man, commonly, receives more income in a year than the total value of his possessions while the rich man's income, being composed largely of rent, interest, and dividends, will, ordinarily, constitute but three to ten per cent of his wealth. Under these circumstances, it is practically inevitable that income distribution must approach much closer to the line of equality than does the curve of wealth.

It was shown in a previous chapter that there was a marked similarity in the relative distribution of wealth in Wisconsin to that in Prussia and France. It likewise seems interesting to compare the distribution of income in the United States with that of a European country. Prussia is the only important nation of Europe publishing income statistics in a convenient form for analysis. A considerable amount of estimating was necessary, especially in the case of the lowest income class, in order to reduce the statistics to a form in which comparison was possible. It is believed, however, that Tables XLV and XLVI approximate the truth rather closely. If the estimates are correct, the curves illustrating the relative

TABLE XLV

THE ESTIMATED DISTRIBUTION OF INCOME AMONG THE PRUSSIAN POPULATION IN 1910.[1]				
Income in Marks Per Family.	Number of Persons in Families of Given Income.	Income of Entire Class in Millions of Marks.	Percentage of Total Population.	Percentage of Total Amount of Income.
Less than 900	17,203,000	4,732[2]	42.84	20.75
900 and under 1,500 .	15,123,000	6,435	37.66	28.21
1,500 " " 3,000 .	5,470,000	3,982	13.62	17.46
3,000 " " 6,500	1,558,000	2,076	3.88	9.10
6,500 " " 9,500 .	289,000	735	.72	3.22
9,500 " " 30,500 .	402,000	2,035	1.00	8.92
30,500 " " 100,000 .	96,000	1,566	.24	6.87
100,000 and over	16,000	1,247	.04	5.47
Totals...............	40,157,000	22,808	100.00	100.00

distributions of income in Prussia and the United States bear as close a resemblance to each other as did those for the same nations which portrayed the distribution of wealth. This gives additional evidence in support of the theory that the relative distribution of wealth and income is dependent rather upon the laws governing industry than upon the geography or natural resources of the country concerned. This is indicated by the fact that the relative distribution is very similar in Prussia to that in the United States while, at the same time, Prussia is, absolutely,

[1] Estimated from *Die Zeitschrift des königlichen preussischen statistischen Landesamts, 1911,* pp. 4, 8–10, xlvi–xlvii.

[2] Average income per family assumed to be 750 marks.

extremely poor both in wealth and income as compared to its American neighbors. The comparisons
will be more clearly brought out by reference to
Table XLVII and Figs. 28 and 29.

TABLE XLVI

The Estimated[1] Distribution of Income Among the Prussian Population in 1910.				
Income in Marks per Family.	Thousands of Persons in Families of Given Class.	Amount of Income in Millions of Marks.	Percentage of Total Popula-tion.	Percentage of Total Amount of Income.
Less than 900 .	17,203	4,732	42.84	20.75
" " 1,500 .	32,326	11,167	80.50	48.96
" " 3,000 .	37,796	15,149	94.12[2]	66.42
" " 6,500 .	39,354	17,225	98.00	75.52
" " 9,500 .	39,643	17,960	98.72	78.74
" " 30,500 .	40,045	19,995	99.72	87.66
" " 100,000 .	40,141	21,561	99.96	94.53
100,000 and over .	40,157	22.808	100.00	100.00

For the sake of convenience, the population has
been classified into exactly the same divisions used
in the study of the comparative wealth of the different
nations. Fig. 28 indicates that, while the total
wealth of the United States is vastly greater than
that of Prussia, yet the various relative shares are
remarkably similar, the chief difference being that

[1] Computed from the preceding table.

[2] This is radically different from the figure given by Mr.
Streightoff in the *Columbia University Studies*, Volume LII,
Number 2, p. 81. He there estimates 56 per cent of the families
to receive less than 2,700 marks annual income. It would seem
that the figure should be much nearer 90 per cent.

the lower middle class in Prussia possesses a little smaller fraction and the upper middle class a little larger portion than the corresponding sectors representing the same classes of the population of the United States.

TABLE XLVII

THE MONEY INCOME OF DIFFERENT FRACTIONS OF THE POPULATION IN PRUSSIA AND IN THE UNITED STATES IN 1910.[1]				
Class of Population.	Country.	Percentage of Total Income Received by Class.	Average Income Per Capita in Dollars.	Ratio of Income to that of the same Class in the United States.
Poorest, 65 per cent.	Prussia......	35.8	74	37.8
	United States.	38.6	197	100.0
Lower middle class, 65–80 per cent.	Prussia......	12.7	114	36.4
	United States.	14.2	314	100.0
Upper middle class, 80–98 per cent.	Prussia......	27.0	203	41.0
	United States.	26.8	494	100.0
Richest, 2 per cent.	Prussia......	24.5	1,656	48.9
	United States.	20.4	3,386	100.0
All classes	Prussia......	100.0	135	40.7
	United States.	100.0	332	100.0

The richest fifth of the families in each country claims about half the income—in Prussia the fraction being a trifle more, and in the United States a trifle less.

[1] Computed from Tables XLV and XLVI.

FIGURE 28

TOTAL MONEY INCOME OF THE PEOPLE OF PRUSSIA AND THE
UNITED STATES AS DIVIDED AMONG THE DIFFERENT FRAC-
TIONS OF THE POPULATION.

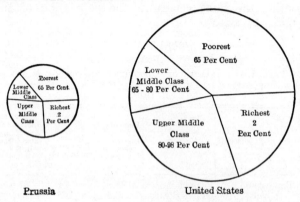

Prussia   United States

AVERAGE INCOMES IN DIFFERENT NATIONS

So much for the similarities. The differences appear when we compare the absolute amounts as is
done in Fig. 29. This illustration shows us that every
fraction of the American people possesses double or
nearly treble the income of the corresponding classes
in Prussia—and yet, we Americans complain greatly
of poverty!

The British Board of Trade reports show that in
the two countries the prices are not materially
different for most articles. House rent and vegetables
are two items that are cheaper in Prussia and with
potatoes to eat and a roof over its head, a family

FIGURE 29

AVERAGE PER CAPITA MONEY INCOME OF EACH FRACTION OF
THE POPULATION IN PRUSSIA AND THE UNITED STATES

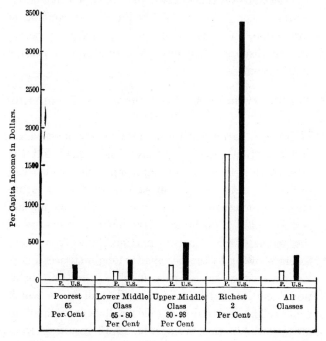

can live. Yet, Prussia is not counted one of the poor
nations of Europe. Austria, Russia, Italy, Spain,
and the Balkan States would doubtless make a
much less favorable showing.[1] And what is the reason

[1] Mr. Streightoff estimates in *Columbia University Studies*,
Volume LII, Number 2, p. 87, that 80 per cent of the English
families have incomes of less than £140 or $681. In the United

for their poverty? They have fertile soil, rich mines, and, in most cases, extensive forests. What is lacking? To answer this query is to touch upon the fundamental basis of economic welfare—the control of population, and it is necessary to clear this up before we can discuss intelligently the question of income distribution.

THE RELATION OF AVERAGE INCOME TO POPULATION DENSITY

Given: a nation with a definite supply of resources and a certain stage of progress in science and the arts, there is always a definite population which can utilize these advantages in such a way as to secure maximum average benefits for all. When population is very sparse, too large a fraction of the energy of the people is spent in transporting things from place to place, owing to the necessarily long distances intervening between settlements and the poor transportation facilities which a light traffic will make worth while. The demand for goods will be too small to make possible the savings of effort resulting from large scale production. The people will be too few to enable them to maintain a national government powerful enough to command the respect of other States, according to Table XLIV, 39 per cent have incomes as low as $700. He calculates that 90 per cent in England have less than $1022 per family while, in the United States, our estimates show only about 44 per cent below this mark.

nations. It is impossible to construct imposing public buildings or extensive public improvements. The real income of society is not augmented by the advantages of social life brought about through proximity to one's neighbors. In short, the country suffers from the hardships commonly associated with frontier life.

When, however, the most fertile lands have been largely occupied; when mines are being operated by most modern methods; when magnificent canals and railways make easy the interchange of the various products necessary for civilized comfort; when huge factories, equipped with the latest inventions, turn out multitudinous products; when the government is strong and powerful enough to afford protection against foreign foes; then, an increase of population merely means a decrease in the general welfare. If more people must be supported, poorer lands must be utilized; mines must be dug deeper and poorer grades of ore extracted; the cities become more and more crowded; and, in accordance with the well-known law of diminishing returns, less and less real income is obtained in exchange for an hour's labor by the average man. The density of population which a spacious nation like the United States needs in order to secure the maximum per capita real income is not great. The bringing into cultivation of poorer lands and the operation of less productive mines indicates, in general, economic retrogression rather than progress. Under these circumstances, the only gain from large numbers is that the government is enabled to raise a larger army, and even this military gain is partially offset by the decrease in financial ability resulting from the poverty of the people. Besides, the crowding of the inhabitants breeds discontent and desire for the conquest of new territory, thus often leading to war when, otherwise, peace would prevail. It should, therefore, be the aim of every nation to keep its population at that number which is found to result in the greatest amount of real income to the average citizen. As a nation grows older and its natural resources are depleted, the population should be correspondingly decreased unless, in the meantime, the increasing difficulties of securing nature's treasures have been offset by newly discovered methods of extraction. The constant increase of population going on in the crowded nations of the globe is, therefore, directly in opposition to the welfare of their people. The facts, then, which should be clearly kept in mind are:

1. **Every nation should maintain its numbers at that point found to give the maximum average real income.**

2. **Natural resources are beyond human control; therefore, population is the factor in which, necessarily, the required adjustment should take place.**

Human history, however, shows that these rules, so essential to the general welfare, have rarely been comprehended—much less carried into effect. Even yet, the majority of people, including some economists, believe population to be something beyond control the regulation of which must be left to the tender mercies of Fate. Efforts are made almost wholly in the direction of stretching further the gifts of nature. In China, the forests have been stripped from the mountains, the lowlands have been diked, the swamps drained, and still, when floods do come or when the crops are a little short, the people die like flies during a frost. This is the result of the failure to recognize the inevitable laws of population. Even in England and the United States we hear a ceaseless clamor that all the land be given to the people. If every great estate, every park, every woodland were opened to cultivation, the people would soon be in worse condition and not better off. The timber supply would be lessened; floods would be more severe; and, worst of all, the scenic beauty— one of Nature's richest gifts to mankind—would be marred or destroyed. It cannot be too strongly emphasized that the setting aside of great areas for parks or pleasure grounds does not, ordinarily, in any way diminish the prosperity of the common people but only lessens their numbers. To see this fact

17

clearly, we must thoroughly understand the laws of population.

It was Thomas R. Malthus who, almost a century ago, clearly set forth those great laws which have been persistently misquoted and railed against, but which have stood like adamant against all attacks and have remained to put to scorn all their assailants. Malthus pointed out that, in all countries in the lower stages of civilization, population was controlled just like the number of weeds in an abandoned field—the weaker ones are choked out until there is room enough for the stronger to survive in comfort. In the past, the great masses of the people of all nations have lived on the **subsistence level.** Three children were born to one that survived. Every crop shortage meant famine and pestilence. Any excess of population died of famine, gained a new food supply by war, or perished in the attempt to secure sustenance. Thus population was fitted to the supply of subsistence by **positive checks,** e. g., war, starvation, disease, and pestilence.

But, he also showed that, in a few of the more enlightened countries and among the better educated classes of the people in many nations, the population was deliberately limited to such an extent as to enable the children not barely to **subsist** but to **live according to a certain standard of comfort** set by the social class of which the parents were members.

A man of the upper classes considered the maintenance of his **standard of living** preferable to marriage and the rearing of children. Under these circumstances, certain **preventive checks** were used to keep the number of children from becoming greater than could be supported in the manner customary to the class to which the parents belonged. In some regions, men were not allowed to marry until there was a vacant house in the village. More commonly, the prevailing opinion of his associates prevented a man marrying until he could assure a wife proper support and late marriages tended towards small families. In many other instances, the number of births was deliberately regulated by the parents.

Malthus went on to show that, as a rule, it was only possible for any nation, or any class of people in a nation, to emerge from the depths of poverty and degradation when they decided to substitute **preventive** for **positive** checks as the method of controlling their numbers.[1] He hoped, but hardly dared to expect, that, some day, even the lower classes—the common working people—would take this tremendous step in advance and thus strike off the shackles which bound them to a life of miserable toil.

A clear comprehension of these principles enables

[1] An admirable article in this connection is that by the able economist, Professor Thomas N. Carver, entitled *How Ought Wealth to be Distributed?* It may be found in the *Atlantic Monthly*, Volume XCVII, p. 727.

us to understand that the regulation of the population
of a nation is not the impossibility that many learned
men have believed it to be. On the contrary, the
numbers tend to be automatically regulated by the
existing stage of culture. Among the uneducated,
lust is the dominant passion and it always tends to
keep the number of mouths to be fed a little larger
than the food supply—in other words a considerable
share of the inhabitants are always starving or on the
verge of starvation. Education, however, works a
revolution. It makes ambition the ruling motive of
men's lives and wealth is necessary in order to satisfy
ambition. To gain wealth and luxury, children must
be few. The average size of the family is reduced to
such an extent that the population is likely to approximate the number required to secure the maximum
per capita income obtainable from the resources of
the region. If, then, migration from without is
prevented, education, alone, acts as an automatic
regulator of the most beneficent and powerful type
and by supplementing its effects to some degree by
eugenic legislation a nation may reasonably be
expected to approach ideal conditions as regards the
number of its people.

Only in the last few decades and in a small number
of the most progressive nations has there been reason
to believe that the dreams of Malthus would yet
come true and that the great common people might

eventually reach that stage of enlightenment in which they would almost universally substitute the **preventive** for the **positive** checks, thus releasing themselves from the bonds of poverty and ushering in a new era of democracy—an era of general prosperity and progress.

From the beginnings of history down nearly to the present time, the overwhelming majority of the people—just like the beasts of the field—have had their numbers governed wholly by **positive** checks, hence have lived on the **subsistence** level. Even yet, most of Asia and large sections of Europe are in this stage of progress. Indeed, we have too large a fraction of the population in our own country who still multiply up to the limits of subsistence.

As has been pointed out, progress is not a continuous possibility as long as this stage of civilization prevails. A people can permanently advance only when it substitutes what Malthus called the **preventive** checks in place of the **positive** checks. True, a nation may occupy new and unsettled territory and, without any restraint on population, for a time grow rich and powerful. But if, in the interim, the standards of living are not so elevated that, when the necessity arises, the size of the family will be limited to that which the family income can support in comfort, nothing can hinder a return to degradation.

We send ship loads of food to China and India to

allay the famine, all unaware that we are simply putting off the inevitable day of starvation for some part of the population. To attempt to better the economic condition of the masses of those nations without lowering their birth rate is as hopeless a task as trying to stamp out typhoid fever while still supplying the people with water laden with the deadly germs. Within reasonable limits, a nation's permanent economic welfare, then, depends but little on whether the soil is rich or sterile, the mines productive or exhausted, but, on the contrary, it is based almost wholly, on the question as to whether the masses of the people have passed over the deep but narrow gulf which separates the control of population by a standard of living from that condition in which it is limited only by the means of subsistence, for it is the crossing of this gulf which substitutes reason in place of the animal instincts.

The fertile wilderness to which our forefathers migrated afforded an almost unparalleled opportunity for the progress of the race. By no possibility, could they overpopulate this vast territory short of several generations. And the riches thus thrust upon them built up new economic ideals—a worthy standard of comfort which, it is to be earnestly hoped, we shall always maintain and improve. The European nations were not so favored and, hence, they have made much less progress in the fight to escape from the chains of want forged by their own uncontrolled passions. The French people have seen the light and placed their numbers on a static basis. In other European nations, the falling birth rate shows that a larger and larger section of the population are crossing the chasm and joining the forces of progress—the great army of democracy which chooses a decent living for its off-spring rather than the rearing of countless millions to perish before the cannon's mouth in the struggle for food. When each nation has learned how to regulate its population in accordance with the resources available for their support, one of the prime reasons for encroaching upon the territories of other powers will have disappeared and a long step will have been taken in the direction of world peace.

And the degree to which a nation has progressed may easily be measured by the poverty or affluence of the common people. China and India, with their fertile plains and valleys, retain their high birth rate and the masses are never far from starvation. In most of Europe, the birth rate is somewhat lower, and the people are beginning to enjoy a few comforts. In the United States, Canada, and Australasia, the native born population has a rigorously controlled birth rate and the people are the most prosperous of the world.

And this leads us back to the subject of the distribution of income in the United States. Fig. 29 shows us that the rich have much while the poor have little. Shall we, then, take from the rich and give to the poor by some roundabout legal process? When discussing wealth, we brought out the fact that the rich were great savers and so accumulated much of the capital which enables the nation to gain a large income to distribute. Any system which threatens to diminish saving is to be looked upon with alarm for its long time effects are certain to be injurious to society at large.

But the rich are great spenders as well as great savers. They waste millions upon millions in wanton display, while the widow and orphan starve a mile from their doors. Is this right? Shall we continue to allow it to go on?

The socialists would solve the problem by letting the government do the saving and abolishing all swollen incomes. This settles the question of the rich. Does it benefit the poor?

The problem of the poor is the vital point of the whole question of distribution. We have always had the poor with us—must we always have them? Table XLVII shows that, in the United States, we produce each year an income of some $332 per capita or about $1,500 per family. If this were equally distributed, none would be in poverty, none would live in affluence. But how long would this condition last? As long as we have any considerable section of our people who have not yet substituted a **high standard of living** for the **subsistence plane,** added income for the poor would merely mean more rapid multiplication of the lowest and least desirable classes. In a few years, the poverty would be as great as before and the average intelligence and prosperity of the whole people would have been greatly reduced.

Of recent years, organized charity has taught us not to distribute alms without careful consideration. The eugenists are just beginning to impress upon us the absurd folly of breeding great troops of paupers, defectives and criminals to be a burden upon organized society.

We may conclude, therefore, without reservation, that to take from the rich and give indiscriminately to the poor would injure and not benefit the nation as a whole. The levelling down process can only be helpful in so far as the income taken from the rich is used to educate and thus stimulate the ambition and elevate the standard of living of the poor. If used merely to increase the wages of the lowest class, the long time effects might, eventually, be no better than to have it spent for steam yachts or million dollar balls.

Of late, we have heard a tremendous demand from would-be social reformers for a "living wage." We hear the employers on all sides denounced as heartless villains because they do not pay enough to allow their employees to live in decency and comfort. But this sentiment seems to arise from a superficial analysis of the difficulty. Why are the employees not in a position to demand a satisfactory return for their services? Whose fault is it? And the ultimate blame must be laid not upon their employers but upon the parents and grandparents of the workers themselves. Why did these ancestors of the present generation bring into the world children whom they could afford neither to educate nor to train for some occupation the products of which were sufficiently in demand to make a living wage easily secured? Why indeed! Simply because these same parents and grandparents were either incompetent, ignorant, or unwilling to restrain their animal passions. Here we have an excellent example of "visiting the iniquity of the father upon the children unto the third and fourth generation." But this fact is not recognized by many of the radical "social uplifters" of the present day and, as a result, we hear American employers and American society in general denounced is unmeasured terms for misdeeds committed across the ocean by men the most of whom are long since in their graves. Yes, we should have a living wage, but we shall not get it by demanding that people pay for a limitless supply of labor which does not know how to produce the articles and services which consumers are willing to buy. The situation may be remedied by scientific treatment of the causes but never by bitter invective and passionate denunciation of those who are not primarily to blame. The price of any sort of labor will go up easily and naturally enough when the supply of that special kind of labor becomes scarce and will go down when more laborers appear on the scene. In this respect, labor does not differ from wheat or steel or cotton. If, therefore, we are desirous of bettering the condition of the workers in poorly paid occupations, we must, in some way, diminish the numbers desiring those kinds of employment. The wages will then take care of themselves.

In the preceding pages, it has been shown that the per capita income of the American people has been increasing steadily and rapidly during the period covered by our study; that it now amounts to the comfortable sum of $1,500 per family but that it is very unequally distributed; that fairly equal distribution is at present impracticable because the lower classes of our population have, as yet, failed to substitute preventive for positive checks in controlling the population supply and the general elevation of the standard of living of these lower classes has been prevented by the rapid multiplication of the defective and incompetent and the still more rapid influx of the ignorant and unprogressive classes of Europeans; that, as a result, a large section of our people still remains in poverty; that the members of the unskilled wage-earning class have, during the last two decades, been compelled to satisfy their needs with a lower rather than a higher real wage; and that, in the meantime, the property holding classes have seen their income in purchasing power continue to increase at a satisfactory rate. And what of the future? Do the coming years promise more and more bounteous returns to the average American? Will our people continue to grow more and more rich and opulent, or are there ominous portents of economic disaster ahead?

The decline in wages measured in purchasing power is not a good omen and the same may be said of the very rapid rise in the relative price of foodstuffs so noticeable in recent years. The importations of corn and beef from Argentina cause us to wonder whether the United States can longer legitimately be called "the larder of the world."

We can scarcely view with absolute complacency the decline in our exports of food products. Meat fell off from $202,236,842 in 1906 to $150,662,633 in 1913. Wheat has gone down from $190,546,305 in 1880 to $89,036,428 in 1913. Corn exports have decreased from $85,206,400 in 1900 to $28,800,544 in 1913. These facts simply indicate that the time is close at hand when the United States will be importing rather than exporting staple foodstuffs. And whence can we hope to draw food supplies for any long period of time? Canada, South America, and Australia are the only sources of moment and they will doubtless be kept busy feeding the teeming millions of Europe and Asia.

It seems very doubtful that there is room for another great nation dependent primarily upon manufacturing for support. Besides, our mineral resources are far from inexhaustible and it is certain to become more and more difficult to extract them from the earth. Our gas wells are ceasing to flow and, in the older fields, the oil wells are nearing exhaustion.

But even more disturbing to our equanimity than the failure of our natural resources to keep pace with our growing numbers is, perhaps, the rise of class antagonism, and the growing disrespect of a considerable section of the laboring people for law and order, this feeling being manifested by riotous strikes, wholesale murders, dynamite outrages and that most contemptible of all modes of attack, *sabotage.*

Under these circumstances, is there any possibility of maintaining our present standard of stability and of prosperity for any great length of time? The answer is, that it is possible, but only upon the condition that the lesson be thoroughly learned that the nation which wishes to progress must keep its population adjusted to its resources and not waste time in the vain attempt to make resources keep pace with a population increasing by leaps and bounds. The latter method, which still seems to be the one commonly thought of as the only available means of staving off famine, is almost as primitive as kindling fire by rubbing two sticks together and is certainly unworthy of the intellectual development and the scientific modes of thought prevalent in the twentieth century. **But poverty should go!** The coming hundred years should see it practically eradicated from the American domain. Whenever we eliminate the section of our population remaining, from the reproductive standpoint, on the low plane of their four-footed ancestors, there seems to be no reason why we cannot so distribute the income that all may secure the needed comforts. With proper educational and eugenic measures, it should be possible to cause this section of our people to be a negligible factor by the year 2000 A.D. But, it must again be remembered that we cannot afford to allow our prosperity to wait until the whole world has advanced to a high plane. This would sacrifice the tremendous advantage which we have already gained and would postpone all real economic progress to some remote future date. We cannot at once educate and reform the benighted of all nations and we cannot reasonably hope to make any progress in draining the swamp of poverty and incompetence in our own land if we continue to pass unnoticed the break in the levee through which is pouring a constant river of illiterate and submerged humanity.[1] True we have done wonders in uplifting the immigrants of past years but the soaring prices of food products, the falling real wages, the growing industrial unrest, all tell us that we are tempting fate too far.

It is time to heed the warnings and take proper measures to guard the citadel of American prosperity against the subtle assaults of the low-standard alien invaders. With American problems alone to solve, there seems to be no apparent reason why we cannot so adjust our population to our resources as to continually increase the average real income of the American citizen and eventually to make **want** a word unknown in the land. But, if we attempt to uplift the downtrodden of the whole earth by sharing with them the food and raiment belonging to our children, we can look for nothing better than the gradual disappearance of our widespread comfort and a slow re-entrance into those sloughs of want and misery from which our ancestors escaped with such great difficulty and from which it may again require many generations of patient effort to emerge. It is ours to decide. Which path will we choose?

[1] One can hardly afford to miss reading in this connection the masterly address by President Frank A. Fetter to the American Economic Association. It is recorded in the Supplement of the *American Economic Review* for March, 1913, p. 5. The address is entitled *Population or Prosperity.*

APPENDIX

TABLE VIA

The Estimated Value of Business Buildings in the United States. (In Millions of Dollars.)					
Census Year.	All Classes of Business Buildings.[5]	Barns and Other Out-buildings on Farms.[1]	Factory.[2]	Mining.[3]	Office, Store, and Miscella-neous.[4]
1850	1,113	550	100	13	450
1860	2,160	1,097	175	38	850
1870	2,975	1,206	288	81	1,400
1880	4,117	1,591	419	107	2,000
1890	5,700	1,912	878	173	2,737
1900	7,250	2,134	1,450	326	3,340[6]
1910	13,301	3,795	2,885	496	6,125

[1] Estimated on the basis that sixty per cent of the value of all farm buildings is in buildings other than residences and that, before 1900, the buildings formed the same proportion of farm value as indicated by the figures for 1910 and 1900.

[2] Assumed to show for each year the same ratio to primary horse-power as shown in 1900.

[3] Assumed to bear the same ratio to the value of the output as shown in 1900.

[4] Assumed to bear the same ratio to the total national income as borne in 1900.

[5] Error for 1900 and 1910 probably not greater than 15 per cent, for other years not greater than 25 per cent.

[6] Half the value of "Other Business Property"—*United States Census of Wealth, Debt, and Taxation, 1904*, p. 17.

TABLE VIʙ

The Estimated Value of Capital Used by Railways and Other Public Utilities in the Continental United States.[1] (In Millions of Dollars.)						
Census Year.	Total.[2]	Steam Railways.	Street and Interurban Railways.	Water, Light and Power.	Telegraphs and Telephones.	Water Transportation.
1850	639	459	4	83	—	93
1860	1,868	1,542	10	157	—	159
1870	3,109	2,669	46	235	10	149
1880	5,386	4,706	100	382	27	171
1890	8,366	7,052	389	580	62	283
1900	10,926	7,680	1,750	950	268	278
1910	23,319	13,600	5,550	2,239	1,210	720

[1] Estimated from numerous Reports and Bulletins of the United States Census.

[2] Error for 1900 and 1910 probably not greater than 10 per cent, for preceding years, not greater than 15 per cent in 1890 or 30 per cent in 1850.

TABLE VIc

THE ESTIMATED VALUE OF THE MOVABLE MACHINERY AND
TOOLS IN USE IN THE CONTINENTAL UNITED STATES.
(In Millions of Dollars.)

CENSUS YEAR.	INDUSTRY.				
	All Industries.[4]	Agri-culture.[1]	Manu-facturing.[2]	Mining.[3]	Miscel-laneous.[3]
1850	399	152	129	28	90
1860	665	246	249	50	120
1870	1,206	337	544	165	160
1880	2,373	406	1,507	260	200
1890	2,665	494	1,584	290	300
1900	4,006	750	2,541	315	400
1910	5,995	1,265	3,795	335	600

[1] Reports of the United States Census.

[2] Estimated as a percentage of the total capital invested. Curve used based on percentages for 1890, 1900 and 1905 as shown by the Census.

[3] Rough estimate.

[4] Error probably not greater than 20 per cent in the last two decades, increasing perhaps to 30 per cent in 1850.

TABLE VIIIA

THE ESTIMATED VALUE OF CONSUMPTION GOODS IN THE CONTINENTAL UNITED STATES.[5] (In Millions of Dollars.)						
Census Year.	Total.	City Residences.[1]	Farm Residences.[2]	Churches, Theatres, etc.[3]	Furniture, Carriages, Automobiles, etc.[4]	Clothing, Personal Ornaments, etc.[4]	Miscellaneous.[4]
1850	2,317	1,271	366	150	350	135	45
1860	4,197	2,016	731	250	800	300	100
1870	5,968	3,029	804	375	1,100	500	160
1880	9,645	5,015	1,060	600	1,900	800	270
1890	15,239	7,794	1,275	970	3,600	1,200	400
1900	20,824	10,021	1,423	1,200	4,880	2,000	1,300
1910	32,976	17,546	2,530	2,200	6,700	3,000	1,000

[1] Estimated on the basis of the Census figures for 1900, assuming residence value to form a constant ratio to the per capita income of the United States times the urban population.

[2] Estimated at 40 per cent of the value of all farm buildings.

[3] Rough estimate.

[4] Estimated as an approximately constant share of total wealth.

[5] The estimates in this table for years preceding 1890 are little more than guesses and are submitted only because no material for more accurate computations seems to be available. The figures for 1900 are probably within 20 per cent of the correct results and those for 1890 and 1910 probably do not err by more than 30 per cent.

TABLE XXXA

Wages and Salaries;

All Returns Ascribed to the Efforts of Employees, by Employments.

(For the Continental United States in Millions of Dollars.)

Employment.	1850.	1860.	1870.	1880.	1890.	1900.	1910.
Government.	64.8	122.8	362.7	411.4	668.8	922.2	1,306.2
Light and power[1]	.5	1.0	1.5	2.0	2.4	11.2	55.0
Fisheries	2.0	2.6	4.0	6.2	10.6	12.0	15.1
Agriculture	93.5	152.8	711.7	669.6	679.8	922.4	1,424.3
Telegraphs and telephones	0	1.0	2.7	6.0	13.5	30.0	117.9
Water transportation	154.3	235.8	165.7	158.7	95.9	102.4	56.2
Street railways	1.0	2.4	7.0	14.0	45.0	73.0	233.0
Railroads	8.9	35.7	111.9	147.4	431.5	570.2	979.0
Mining	13.0	42.0	83.0	113.0	231.0	399.0	698.0
Manufacturing	236.8	378.9	775.6	948.0	2,249.0	2,391.0	4,366.0
Commercial, professional, etc.	218.0	376.1	1,043.7	1,327.3	2,034.3	3,057.3	5,052.9
Total	792.8	1,351.1	3,269.5	3,803.6	6,461.8	8,490.7	14,303.6

[1] Private electric companies.

TABLE XXXв

INTEREST;

VALUE PRODUCT ASCRIBED TO CAPITAL, CLASSIFIED ACCORDING TO THE USE OF THE CAPITAL.

(For the Continental United States, in Millions of Dollars.)

Use of Capital.	1850.	1860.	1870.	1880.	1890.	1900.	1910.
Government	23.7	26.0	49.3	31.3	77.4	364.6	857.1
Light and power[1]	1.6	2.3	3.0	3.7	4.4	16.1	79.5
Fisheries	.7	.8	.9	2.2	2.6	3.0	4.5
Agriculture	127.3	238.1	296.1	347.0	436.0	546.0	934.0
Telegraph and telephones	.0	1.0	2.9	6.6	13.9	20.3	68.8
Water transportation	6.5	11.1	10.4	12.0	19.8	19.4	50.4
Street railways	.4	1.0	5.5	12.4	13.3	53.0	71.5
Railroads	20.8	80.6	152.8	259.0	329.3	404.4	750.2
Manufacturing	43.2	88.0	173.2	458.5	539.1	816.5	1,667.9
Mining	5.6	10.0	33.0	56.0	40.0	73.0	67.0
Commerce, mercantile, residential, etc.	46.7	73.7	137.4	184.5	262.9	379.4	593.0
Total	276.5	532.6	864.5	1,373.2	1,738.9	2,695.7	5,143.9

[1] Private electric companies.

TABLE XXXc

RENT;

VALUE PRODUCT ASCRIBED TO LAND, CLASSIFIED ACCORDING TO THE USE OF THE LAND.

(For the Continental United States, in Millions of Dollars.)

Use of Land.	1850.	1860.	1870.	1880.	1890.	1900.	1910.
Government	11.8	12.9	24.6	15.6	38.7	182.2	428.5
Light and power[1]	.1	.2	.3	.4	.5	2.3	11.4
Fisheries	.0	.0	.1	.1	.1	.2	.2
Agriculture	94.0	193.0	217.0	302.0	404.0	522.0	1,139.0
Water transportation	.2	.3	.3	.3	.5	.5	1.7
Street railways	.1	.3	3.3	7.4	7.9	31.8	42.9
Railroads	3.0	12.0	30.6	51.8	65.9	80.9	150.1
Mining	1.6	5.0	13.0	22.0	38.0	82.0	178.0
Manufacturing	4.0	7.4	14.5	20.9	41.0	52.1	66.4
Mercantile, residential, etc.	55.8	90.1	159.5	221.8	317.2	442.0	655.7
Total	170.6	321.2	463.2	642.3	913.8	1,396.0	2,673.9

[1] Private electric companies.

TABLE XXXd

PROFITS;

ALL RETURNS ASCRIBED TO THE EFFORTS OF ENTREPRENEURS, BY EMPLOYMENT.

(For the Continental United States in Millions of Dollars.)

Employment.	1850.	1860.	1870.	1880.	1890.	1900.	1910.
Light and power[1]	.6	1.1	1.6	2.1	2.6	6.4	31.6
Fisheries	7.3	9.5	10.0	25.3	24.9	27.3	29.1
Agriculture	450.1	504.3	558.4	157.4	740.0	1,697.6	3,344.7
Telegraphs and telephones	.0	1.5	3.8	1.7	3.5	5.1	17.2
Water transportation	213.6	324.4	223.4	210.6	105.6	115.7	—11.4
Street railways	.3	.8	2.2	5.0	5.4	21.2	28.5
Railroads	2.8	10.7	20.4	34.5	43.9	53.9	100.0
Mining	2.8	5.0	16.0	27.0	20.0	37.0	33.0
Manufacturing	147.4	322.1	637.8	367.9	983.3	1,829.7	2,159.8
Commercial, etc.	149.0	251.3	649.3	740.1	1,037.9	1,588.2	2,675.6
Total	973.9	1,430.7	2,122.9	1,571.6	2,967.1	5,382.1	8,408.1

[1] Private electric companies.

TABLE XXXIIa

			NUMBER OF EMPLOYEES IN THOUSANDS.		
CENSUS YEAR.	TOTAL NUMBER IN THOUSANDS.	NUMBER OF ENTREPRENEURS IN THOUSANDS.	All Employees.	Salaried Persons.	Wage Workers.
1850	6,080	2,200	3,880	300	3,580
1860	8,240	3,150	5,090	520	4,570
1870	12,510	4,270	8,240	810	7,430
1880	17,390	5,600	11,790	1,260	10,530
1890	23,320	7,100	16,220	1,850	14,370
1900	29,070	8,720	20,350	3,190	17,160
1910	37,550[2]	9,350	28,200	5,950	22,250

ESTIMATED DISTRIBUTION OF PERSONS GAINFULLY EMPLOYED IN THE CONTINENTAL UNITED STATES.[1]

[1] Estimated principally from the *Census of 1900, Occupations*, Chap. 2.

[2] *Thirteenth Census of the United States*, Volume 4, Table I. Recorded numbers reduced by 617,000 on account of probable errors mentioned on pages 28 and 29 of this Census volume.

TABLE XXXVIA

Indices of the Price of Labor Per Hour for Female Wage Earners in Important Manufacturing Industries.[1]						
Weight.	21	9	2	3	5	2
Industry.	All In-dustries.	Cotton.	Woolen.	Silk.	Knit Goods.	Boots and Shoes.
Year.						
1890	100.0	99.4	98.6	96.4	104.9	97.6
1891	99.5	98.9	98.3	94.5	106.2	94.5
1892	99.6	98.2	99.7	100.5	102.0	98.3
1893	102.1	104.1	104.5	103.1	97.4	101.3
1894	98.9	99.0	95.5	103.7	95.6	102.6
1895	99.7	98.7	96.1	101.7	100.6	102.0
1896	103.0	105.2	100.0	103.2	100.4	102.3
1897	100.2	102.0	100.6	98.2	97.6	101.9
1898	98.9	98.1	104.1	100.0	97.3	99.6
1899	97.4	96.6	103.6	98.6	94.6	99.6
1900	104.3	109.4	110.4	99.4	96.2	102.8
1901	106.3	110.4	111.5	100.5	101.3	104.3
1902	111.3	113.9	114.3	102.4	113.7	104.2
1903	115.0	117.6	116.7	108.4	115.7	110.0
1904	114.3	117.5	117.0	107.2	113.6	109.5
1905	117.6	120.7	118.6	107.7	118.9	113.8
1906	125.4	131.5	125.5	110.1	126.3	118.4
1907	136.7	148.7	135.2	119.6	131.9	121.7
1908	135.2	147.5	126.5	114.8	134.3	121.3
1909	133.5	142.4	126.9	115.8	135.6	125.2
1910	137.5	148.5	132.1	120.3	135.0	125.3
1911	137.7	148.4	131.6	122.0	135.1	125.9
1912	147.8	164.2	148.3	124.0	140.3	128.0
Av. money wage per hour, 1890–1899	$0.1061	$0.0881	$0.1202	$0.1232	$0.1029	$0.1551
Av. money wage per hour, 1912	0.1541	.1446	.1783	.1528	.1444	.1985

[1] All figures computed from *Bulletins 128 and 134 of the United States Bureau of Labor Statistics.*

TABLE XXXVIIA

INDICES[1] OF THE PRICE OF LABOR PER HOUR FOR MALE WAGE EARNERS IN MANUFACTURING INDUSTRIES.[2]						
Weight.[3]	52	4	1	1	1	3
Industry.	All Industries.	Cotton.[4]	Woolen.[4]	Silk.[4]	Knit Goods.[5]	Boots and Shoes.[5]
Year.						
1890	102.1	108.9	99.8	98.5	107.8	98.7
1891	101.7	102.1	100.9	96.7	109.1	98.3
1892	101.5	100.5	101.8	97.4	94.8	99.6
1893	102.0	105.6	106.0	96.2	109.1	100.4
1894	97.2	97.5	95.4	99.9	100.2	99.0
1895	97.7	96.1	95.6	101.4	110.0	101.2
1896	98.7	102.4	97.6	103.3	95.7	100.0
1897	98.2	97.6	99.1	104.0	91.4	100.4
1898	98.9	94.7	101.3	100.7	93.4	100.7
1899	101.9	94.8	102.2	101.4	88.7	102.4
1900	105.6	106.0	111.2	102.3	92.8	104.4
1901	108.3	106.2	111.5	102.4	104.2	104.1
1902	113.1	112.3	115.5	101.8	102.2	109.0
1903	117.6	118.9	118.6	102.2	123.9	114.1
1904	116.6	115.3	114.3	104.2	118.9	118.9
1905	119.3	118.3	118.9	105.4	123.3	121.5
1906	125.6	131.3	127.7	107.2	128.9	122.7
1907	131.3	148.6	133.5	107.7	138.2	129.7
1908	127.8	146.4	129.7	110.7	131.8	126.6
1909	128.8	141.1	131.9	111.3	129.4	131.8
1910	135.1	143.8	133.0	112.2	137.2	130.8
1911	136.5	147.4	135.1	113.0	138.1	133.2
1912	140.3	162.3	149.1	117.8	154.8	134.1
Av. money price per hour,						
1890–1899	$0.1959	$0.1063	$0.1562	$0.1806	$0.1388	$0.2451
Av. 1912	.2749	.1725	.2330	.2128	.2148	.3288

[1] Base 1890–1899.

[2] Computed from the reports of the United States Bureau of Labor. Occupations and industries weighted according to the approximate number of males employed in 1910.

[3] Weighted approximately according to the number of males employed in 1900, according to the *Census of Occupations.*

[4] *Bulletin 128, United States Department of Labor.*

[5] *Bulletin 134, United States Department of Labor.*

TABLE XXXVIIA (CONT'D)

INDICES OF THE PRICE OF LABOR PER HOUR FOR MALE WAGE EARNERS IN MANUFACTURING INDUSTRIES.

Weight.	14	11	2	2	7	6
Industry.	Hand Trades.[6]	Lumber.[7]	Mill-work.[7]	Furni-ture.[7]	Railroad Cars.[8]	Iron and Steel.[9]
Year.						
1890	99.1	101.9	99.2	100.5	101.6	109.0
1891	99.6	101.4	100.4	101.5	101.4	109.0
1892	100.9	101.5	100.1	102.5	101.7	106.0
1893	100.5	99.9	100.0	101.1	107.0	102.0
1894	98.2	96.7	97.0	99.4	97.5	93.0
1895	98.4	97.0	98.1	97.9	97.3	95.0
1896	99.5	97.4	99.3	97.7	98.0	97.0
1897	100.0	97.7	100.0	100.2	98.4	93.0
1898	100.7	101.5	101.7	98.0	97.8	93.0
1899	103.1	104.5	104.1	102.0	99.5	103.0
1900	107.1	105.4	105.9	102.4	100.6	111.0
1901	111.1	108.6	108.6	107.3	101.7	114.0
1902	116.5	112.1	112.5	114.1	105.4	122.0
1903	121.8	114.2	116.5	115.2	108.9	128.0
1904	123.0	112.3	115.7	117.5	112.2	117.0
1905	124.9	116.3	116.7	121.0	112.7	121.0
1906	131.2	124.4	120.6	125.7	115.3	128.0
1907	136.6	129.6	124.5	127.3	119.4	131.0
1908	138.7	118.7	123.4	127.5	118.5	121.8[10]
1909	141.3	121.6	124.9	126.7	115.9	122.5[10]
1910	146.3	130.0	127.8	130.5	126.2	133.0[10]
1911	149.1	129.9	129.0	132.1	127.9	133.5[10]
1912	151.8	131.5	132.3	135.1	129.0	135.2[10]
Av. money price per hour, 1890–1899	$0.2794	$0.1384	$0.1928	$0.1674	$0.2037	$0.1623
Av. 1912	.4242	.1820	.2551	.2261	.2627	.2195

[6] *Bulletin 131 of the United States Bureau of Labor.*
[7] *Bulletin 129 of the United States Bureau of Labor.*
[8] *Bulletin 137 of the United States Bureau of Labor.*
[9] Wesley Mitchell.   *Business Cycles*, p. 133.
[10] *Bulletin 151 of the United States Bureau of Labor.*

INDEX

271

19